PENSION PONZI

How Public Sector Unions are Bankrupting Canada's Health Care, Education and Your Retirement

BILL TUFTS & LEE FAIRBANKS

John Wiley & Sons Canada, Ltd.

Library and Archives Canada Cataloguing in Publication

Tufts, Bill, 1959-
  Pension Ponzi : how public sector unions are bankrupting Canada's health care, education and retirement / Bill Tufts, Lee Fairbanks.

Also issued in electronic formats.
ISBN 978-1-1180987-3-8

1. Civil service—Canada—Pensions. 2. Debts, Public—Canada. 3. Canada—Economic policy—1991-. I. Fairbanks, Lee, 1954- I. Title.

JL111.S3T83 2011   331.25'29135171   C2011-906101-5

ISBN: 978-1-118-09988-9 (ePub); 978-1-118-09986-5 (eMobi); 978-1-118-09987-2 (ePDF)

Production Credits
Cover design: Adrian So
Cover photo credit: Thinkstock
Interior design: Thomson Digital
Typesetter: Thomson Digital
Printer: Solisco-Tri-Graphic Printing Ltd.

Editorial Credits
Executive Editor: Karen Milner
Production Editor: Jeremy Hanson-Finger
John Wiley & Sons Canada, Ltd.
6045 Freemont Blvd.
Mississauga, Ontario
L5R 4J3

Printed in Canada
1 2 3 4 5 SOL TRI 15 14 13 12 11

ENVIRONMENTAL BENEFITS STATEMENT

John Wiley & Sons - Canada saved the following resources by printing the pages of this book on chlorine free paper made with 100% post-consumer waste.

TREES	WATER	ENERGY	SOLID WASTE	GREENHOUSE GASES
35	34 333	55	4 340	11 282
FULLY GROWN	GALLONS	MILLION BTUs	POUNDS	POUNDS

Environmental impact estimates were made using the Environmental Paper Network Paper Calculator. For more information visit www.papercalculator.org.

CONTENTS

FOREWORD

By Catherine Swift, President, Canadian Federation of Independent Business

The demographic tsunami that has already hobbled many European countries and U.S. states is just starting to hit Canada. Pension and benefit promises that have been made over the past several decades by both private corporations and governments to employees are now coming due as the baby boomers retire, and there has not been anywhere near sufficient money put aside to pay these obligations.

As private sector companies have struggled to remain competitive in the marketplace, they have already, in recent years, scaled back pensions and benefits, or risked facing bankruptcy. As governments do not have to compete in the same manner, and are, in fact, the one "business" that can force "customers" to pay by law via taxes, they have had the ability to procrastinate on this issue even longer than have private sector players.

The end result is that Canadian taxpayers now owe hundreds of billions of dollars in pensions and benefits that governments have already promised, but never put aside the funds to pay for. If governments had been honest and funded these plans properly from the outset, protests from private sector taxpayers would have been so strong that the situation would not have been permitted to become so unbalanced in the first place, with public sector workers now earning much more in compensation and benefits than their private sector counterparts, and retiring much earlier with very generous pensions and other benefits.

With the baby boom generation starting to retire, the chickens are coming home to roost. *Pension Ponzi* outlines how this predicament came into being, how extensive and outrageous Canada's national pension liability situation currently is, and what needs to be done before we destroy our economy and effectively bankrupt the taxpayers who are being asked to pay for this enormous shortfall.

A warning: All Canadians who read this book will be enraged at how, over the decades, our governments have duped us all and built up a massive debt that is now coming due. But all Canadians *should* read this book in order to become informed about this complex issue, and realize the need for all of us to demand of our politicians, at all levels, that it be addressed with the utmost urgency.

INTRODUCTION

Canadians are blissfully unaware that Canada's economic system is broken, defrauded by the most successful economic organization in history—the public sector union. The truth is, our politicians have been coerced by public sector unions into paying salary and benefits packages far beyond what our economy can support, as well as guaranteeing to pay inflated pensions to those same workers after retirement. As the *National Post* said, these giant public pension funds are "wealth confiscated by governments . . . using money taxed from all their constituents."[1] Almost every government employee—*including* elected politicians—will benefit from these pensions, at the expense of the vast majority of Canadians.

The 20 per cent of the workforce that belongs to public sector unions—civil servants, teachers, firefighters, police officers, armed forces personnel, and all government workers, including politicians—have quietly negotiated the most lucrative compensation packages in history. And these will all be paid for with tax dollars—and massive government debt. The CFIB Wage Watch Report[2] shows public sector salaries and benefits exceed those of private industry by up to 30 per cent. More troubling is the fact that their guaranteed, indexed-to-inflation pensions are creating two classes of retirees.

This book will open your eyes to one of the greatest reallocations of legal assets in the history of the world. Some call it pension envy, some call it pension apartheid, some call it fraud. We call it a pension Ponzi plan, an unsustainable scheme to funnel money from one group of Canadians to another under the pretense of providing services. Who will be the loser when it collapses, as all Ponzi schemes eventually do? Consider these facts:

- The Ontario Teachers' Pension Plan (OTPP)[3] has $107.5 billion in assets to fund 295,000 teacher pensions ($366,000 per retiree); the

Ontario Municipal Employees Retirement System (OMERS)[4] has $53 billion for 400,000 members ($120,000 per retiree); and the Canada Pension Plan (CPP)[5] has only $148 billion for 18,000,000 working Canadians ($722 per retiree). The OTPP, believe it or not, is actually $35 billion short[6] of being able to pay its commitments, while OMERS is $8–$9 billion short.[7] The extent of the CPP shortfall is unknown. These shortfalls must be covered by increased taxes yet to come.

- The average CPP benefit payment is $5,919 per year. The average annual pension for a new OTPP retiree, in 2010, is around $42,900 per year.

- The City of Hamilton[8] has a $1.5 billion-yearly budget but an underfunded pension and employee benefits liability of $262 million. The University of Toronto[9] pension funds have deficits estimated to be in excess of $2 billion. These deficit stories are repeated across the country, creating billions of dollars of hidden liabilities. Because these pensions are guaranteed by you, as a taxpayer, the shortfalls will have to be covered either by future taxes or service cuts to health care, education, and other government programs.

- Combined federal and provincial debt now totals more than $1.2 trillion,[10] most of it created by paying public service employees unrealistic wages and making allocations to their pensions. How will the next generation react when it is forced to repay this debt?

- Canada's total government per capita debt alone in 2010 was USD $36,000.[11] This is before liabilities on the Canada Pension Plan or future healthcare costs are estimated. Compare this with the USD per capita debt of the so-called PIIGS group of failing economies: Portugal ($17,000); Italy ($39,000); Ireland ($35,000); Greece ($35,000); and Spain ($17,000).[12] Greece has already defaulted on its pensions, public employee paycheques, and international debt obligations. Will Canada be next?

- Compare the numbers above with the USD per capita debt of the so-called BRIC countries leading a global economic boom in emerging nations: Brazil ($5,800); Russia ($834); India ($695);

and China ($673).[13] Which nations do you think are poised to be winners in the next decade?

- In Canada today there are five employees for every pensioner. By 2036 there will be only two and a half workers—a 50 per cent relative decline in taxpayers, who will be stuck paying for a 100 per cent increase in pensioners living 50 per cent longer.[14] How is this viable?

- Counting on your employer to fund your retirement? Nortel's pension plan is $2.4 billion in deficit,[15] Air Canada's pension fund has a deficit of $2.1 billion,[16] U.S. Steel (formerly Stelco) pensions were cut by 15 per cent, and the government is refusing to top up these funds—or any private pensions that go bust.

- Got your retirement funds invested? Mutual fund withdrawals have led to stagnant returns on the Toronto Stock Exchange (TSE) for the past 10 years, and net losses since 2008[17]—no gains at all while inflation and higher taxes rob you of your buying power. Meanwhile, public employee pension plans invested in the market have their losses covered by your tax dollars. Their returns are guaranteed by your future tax increases.

- The C.D. Howe Institute[18] compared private and public sector workers each earning $50,000. They compared an example of a private sector worker retiring with $255,000 in his Registered Retirement Savings Plan (RRSP), while the same public sector worker will have in excess of $1 million to fund his pension. The public sector worker's RRSPs are built on tax-free benefits and excessive salaries paid with taxpayer dollars. The public sector has accumulated $800 billion into pension plans; the remaining 80 per cent of Canadians have accumulated around $700 billion in RRSPs.

Canada's baby boomers, the country's largest demographic group, account for one-third of our adult population and are moving into their retirement, expecting to live for another 30 years. This is a group that has consistently spent money it should have been saving for its future on fun and games today. No savings, small RRSPs, big mortgages, high credit card balances. The promise they believe has been made to them over a lifetime of financial contribution and achievement is that they will enjoy a quality of life in retirement second to none. The unfortunate truth is far different than that promise.

It's true that some baby boomers—those who have toiled in public service—will have pensions unlike any seen before. These gold-plated retirement packages typically guarantee employees 70 per cent of their highest five years of working income, indexed to inflation, until the day they die. But only 20 per cent of working baby boomers belong to this select group. Another 30 per cent of boomers have some form of private industry and/or personal plans in place to augment their government pensions, but nothing close to those of their public sector counterparts. The majority of the other 50 per cent of boomers will risk living in or near poverty, the equity they created in this country drawn off on a yearly basis to fund public service pensions. These disproportionate public service pensions are funded by taxes, which means that supporting them will divert money from every aspect of government-funded programs, including health care, education, infrastructure, the military, and foreign aid, and will ultimately undermine the quality of life of every Canadian.

Private company pension funds are in deficit, the economy will be stagnant for years to come, jobs are going overseas, the health care system is crumbling. Meanwhile, one group of retiring Canadians is set to raid the public treasury for billions of dollars in guaranteed, indexed pensions. How will the other boomers survive their old age? Consider the following illustration to see just how different your retirement may be from your neighbours'.

Which Future Will be Yours?

Mark and Jennifer lived next door to Carl and Marnie for 32 years. They raised their families in comfortable, three-bedroom homes in a suburb just outside of Toronto. All things considered both couples had a pretty great life. They had regular holidays, late model cars, went out to dinner together often, were subscribers to first-run theatre, belonged to the same golf and country club, bought quality clothes, and didn't worry much about the price of food. Both families had two children, and all of them went to university. Mark and Jennifer have four grandchildren, while Carl and Marnie have three.

Carl and Mark were both accountants by trade, earning their certified public accountant designation within a year of each other. Mark got a job in the accounting department of the local municipality and worked his way through the public service, eventually taking a position with the Canada Revenue Agency. Jennifer worked at the library as an assistant librarian. Carl worked as an accountant for a large steel company for 27 years, but was downsized and let go with a two-year-income severance package when he was 54. He was unable to find similar employment and spent his last 10 working years largely self-employed, doing contract work and income tax returns. Marnie worked part-time while the children were young, and then as a secretary at a law office for 24 years. She retired when the senior law partners took early retirement and the younger lawyers chose not to continue her employment. She was 58 at the time.

For the first 20 years or so, the family incomes coming into the two homes were quite similar but then a gap appeared and continued to widen each year. As a government employee, Mark's income was negotiated by the Canadian Union of Public Employees (CUPE) and outpaced inflation, whereas the manufacturing company that Carl worked for had had a very weak decade starting in the late '90s. Salaries were frozen for several years and a lot of the perks, such as company car allowances and expense accounts, were cut back.

Jennifer also benefited from steady raises negotiated by her union, whereas Marnie was never very good at asking for more money and consequently received small and erratic increases in pay. After Carl lost his job the difference in the couples' incomes accelerated, and when Marnie was fired her income dropped to zero. It's fair to say that Carl and Marnie were caught unprepared for this turn of events. They had both been hard-working, loyal employees and just assumed that they would work at their respective companies until they were 65.

"I suppose as an accountant you might think that I would have seen it coming," says Carl, "but after a while you get used to seeing a bad balance sheet and that becomes the new reality. The company had cut a lot of expenses—I had actually helped them decide which ones to cut—and that included downsizing the workforce. I just never thought they would get rid of senior staff.

"We closed down whole sections of the plant and sent jobs overseas to cut back on wages. We delayed replacement of a lot of our older production equipment and cut back on research and development, but it still wasn't enough. At the end of the day our Canadian labour costs were killing us. Our plant workers were all unionized and we had paid top wages for many, many years but once the steel industry went global we just couldn't compete.

"Our health care costs were killing us too. The average age of our employees was much higher than that of our competitors overseas, and our workers were becoming less productive and less healthy. Our health care premiums jumped every year and there was no end in sight for that. When we started to pay out more in pensions than we were paying our active workforce, there wasn't anywhere to turn."

Once they had absorbed the shock of being fired, Carl and Marnie searched for similar jobs in their fields but were never able to secure permanent positions. They found themselves competing with much younger candidates, usually being interviewed by managers who were much their juniors and had little or no interest in hiring two older workers looking for a short-term bridge to their retirement years. The loss of income caused both Carl and Marnie to stop contributing to their RRSPs, and once they had spent all of Carl's severance money, were forced to draw from their RRSPs well before their 65th birthdays.

Mark and Jennifer, on the other hand, fulfilled the mandates of their employment contracts and were able to retire early with full benefits. Mark retired at 56, having worked 30 years, and Jennifer retired two years later. While they were working, their incomes never stopped increasing. Their incomes weren't affected by the recession in the early '80s, the market crash in the late '90s, the Silicon Valley bust last decade, or the financial market meltdown in 2008. After his official "retirement" as a full-time employee, Mark took contract work with the agency and continued to work while collecting his pension.

Mark and Jennifer's RRSPs did, of course, suffer fluctuations in value based on the stock market, but they had always considered these RRSPs to be an "add-on" to their government-guaranteed pensions anyway, so the loss was really only a paper one. They didn't need this money to live on, and had no plans to redeem any RRSPs until they were forced by government legislation to do so. They were able to leave their money invested and wait to see if the markets rebounded. Truth is, they were hoping to leave this money to their children and grandchildren, or to cash it in and spend it on their offspring while they were still alive.

It was a shock to the couple when Carl and Marnie informed them that they were selling their house and moving into a small condo in a new subdivision about 50 kilometres away. They had always planned to spend their retirement years as neighbours, continuing to borrow each other's tools, share summer barbecues beside the pool, and grow old together as best friends.

"I felt as if my life were somehow ending and would never be the same again. So many memories came to me," says Marnie. "That house was my life, it held my family. It's hard to describe if you've never been through it, but it just seemed so un-Canadian to me to be forced out of my house because of money. Carl and I were good people. We worked hard all our lives, we were honest, and we sure paid a tonne of taxes. I just feel like we tried to do everything we were supposed to do and in the end the system just kicked us out like our lives didn't even matter."

Ten Years Later: Carl and Marnie

The first few years in their new home had not been as difficult as Carl and Marnie feared. There had been a period of adjustment to the smaller rooms, the lack of a backyard, the isolation of not really knowing their neighbours—which was a dramatic change in their day-to-day lives and routines—but they encouraged themselves by pointing out that they still had their health and each other.

Before Carl had been terminated at work, he and Marnie had been overextending their credit like most baby boomers. They had remortgaged their home to access cash for investments and run up credit cards for holidays, a small home theatre room in the basement, a kitchen renovation with beautiful new appliances, and really just living slightly beyond their means. It seems that pretty much every boomer family was living that way in the 1990s and in the first seven or eight years of the new millennium. With both of them unemployed, the couple found it very difficult to pay their bills. They remortgaged their house again to consolidate their loans and hoped that their investments would do well, but when the stock market crashed in 2008 they lost half of their equity. When they finally sold their house, paid off their short-term debts, and reinvested in their condo they had nothing left from their lifetime savings, investments, or RRSPs.

After 10 years in the condo, most of the couple's furniture had become worn and had to be replaced. They had to buy another used car when their old one became unreliable. They had initially tried to continue their previous lifestyle as best they could, taking an annual holiday in the south, renewing their theatre subscription, playing golf. They rationalized that they would not live forever and that their health might start to diminish, so they might as well spend the money while they were able to enjoy it, but now in their early 70s, Carl and Marnie were beginning to realize that they could no longer maintain their lives at this level. Their nest egg was gone; they had maxed out their credit cards and used a $50,000 line of credit on their home.

Carl and Marnie qualified for almost the maximum Canada pension and old-age security payments, but with property taxes going up every year, the price of gas, food, and utilities, and more money being spent for health-related expenses that were not covered by Canada's universal health system (chiropractic adjustments, orthotics, glasses, dental visits), there was nothing left over at the end of the month for luxury items, and even staples were becoming more and more difficult to afford. They began to buy lower-quality meats, store-brand products, and damaged produce, and became the "coupon clippers" they had made fun of before.

The couple found themselves seeing less and less of Mark and Jennifer. Their inability to cover their share of meals, theatre tickets, and other entertainment costs made them feel that they were taking advantage of their friends when they went out together. Much as they tried to stay positive about their lives it became impossible not to feel somewhat jealous of Mark and Jennifer, and eventually that jealousy began to turn into resentment. Carl and Marnie felt they had both contributed so much to their community, and yet their reward was so meagre compared to that of their friends.

Ten Years Later: Mark and Jennifer

Mark and Jennifer's life as seniors turned out to be everything they could have ever imagined, and probably more. They kept their family house and it was a great joy to them to be able to have their children and grandchildren come and stay with them on a regular basis throughout the year. The summers were especially wonderful, and the whole family enjoyed lounging around the big pool in the backyard and frequent barbecues, complete with steak, chicken, fresh fruit, and fine wines.

When Carl and Marnie hit hard times, Mark and Jennifer took this as a warning and paid off their mortgage and credit card debts before they retired. With two government pensions bringing in 70 per cent of their previous working incomes and reduced expenses, they had money left over every month. Each year they planned a special event or major purchase that increased their enjoyment of life. One year they took all their grandchildren to Disney World. Another year they rented three luxury cottages in Muskoka for two weeks and took their entire family on holiday. It was a summer of memories which they would never forget.

"I think we'd have to say that for us, Canada is the best country in the world," says Jennifer. "I guess we were just lucky to have picked careers in government jobs. I can't say we really planned it that way, it just kind of happened. When we started in our jobs they weren't particularly high paid, and neither of us were thinking too much about pensions anyway since we were so young, but our unions did a great job for us and we're just so very grateful for it, especially when you look at what happened to Carl and Marnie."

Mark had always had a passion for vehicles of all kinds and bought himself a high-end, European convertible sports car for the summers. Jennifer preferred a larger vehicle—safer, she called it—and leased a new SUV every four years. They invested in a number of vacation property programs and typically spent between six and eight weeks of the winter in Florida or the Caribbean islands.

For Jennifer's 65th birthday Mark surprised her with a three-week trip to Europe, something she had always wanted. They spent a week in London, a week in Paris, and several days touring Italy. So, all in all, they would be the first to admit that their lives just seemed to get better and better, and that their retirement years truly were the golden years of their lives.

Carl and Marnie's story is not unique. Some 70 per cent of Canadians will have this or much, much less to look forward to when they retire. Carl and Marnie were fortunate to have maintained enough equity in their home to purchase the condo and supplement their pension income into their 70s.

Jennifer and Mark's situation is also not unusual in the sense that some 20 per cent of Canadians are looking forward to a retirement fully funded by your taxes. Perhaps the question is not *how* did this happen, but *why* did this happen? And second to that, is this a fair result in a fair society? Do we believe that Jennifer's work organizing books in a library was more important than Marnie's work helping people deal with their legal issues?

Does Mark deserve a better retirement than Carl because he handled government money, whereas Carl spent his life helping to manage a company that provided jobs for thousands of employees? Who makes these value judgments? Anyone? Who designed this economic system? Anyone, or did it just evolve organically? What will happen to our country when 5 million voting baby boomers discover this inequity in the pension system? What will happen when the next generation of Canadians realizes that the prosperity of their families is being undermined by the billions of dollars being paid to retired public sector workers?

If you are one of the lucky few expecting this kind of guaranteed pension-for-life, we suggest you keep your fingers crossed. The chances that our government will be able to withstand the fury of millions of seniors living near the poverty level—and the anger of millions of working Canadians whose taxes are being redirected into your pockets to allow you to benefit from the wanton and reckless spending of the previous governments you elected—is slim, to say the least.

You might well ask how governments could have let this happen. How did becoming a teacher, a police officer, a public works truck driver, or a municipal office secretary become so much more important to Canada's welfare than being a lawyer, a plumber, a steelworker, or the owner of one of the many thousands of small businesses that are the backbone of Canada's economy? This book will expose the startling truth about our future, show you how we got into this mess, and offer advice about what you can do (if anything) to put yourself on the right side of this life-altering trend.

1

THE ELEPHANT IN THE ROOM

The whole idea of the pension was to provide public servants with a decent retirement when they left public service. It was not to enrich them or to make them wealthy, to allow them to retire younger, with more money, to go off and play golf while the rest of us supported them. This attitude is growing out there in the public. People are beginning to realize what has been done and they are not happy about it.

Jack Dean, PensionTsunami.com

If you happen to be one of the lucky 20 per cent of Canadians who is a government employee, we have to say congratulations. Your employee unions have consistently negotiated phenomenally lucrative contracts on your behalf over the past 30 years—while complaining bitterly that it's never enough. It used to be that government service workers such as librarians, garbage collectors, municipal office staff, and even politicians were paid less than private industry employees doing similar tasks. Partly this was because government workers had better job security, and never had to worry about their employer going out of business or being unable to meet payroll. Partly it was the concept of being a "good citizen," and that the joy of working on behalf of everyone else had some intrinsic value to it. Choosing a career as a teacher, nurse, or police officer had intangible rewards of increased respect and prestige, which offset lower income levels. All that, however, has changed.

It may have started at the politicians' level. If you have been paying attention during the past 30 years, you'll remember a move to raise the salaries of politicians, supposedly in order to attract a higher calibre of person to public office. The theory was that our elected politicians came from an income class populated by people with low moral and educational standards, who were prone to corruption, bribes and influence peddling, and poor decision making. The idea was that the type of people we needed to run our country were highly sought after by business and had the opportunity to make more money there, and that we therefore needed to match incomes with business or at least offer an attractive benefits package to encourage such people to commit to public service.

We will leave it to you to decide if our current crop of politicians demonstrates a higher ethical and moral standard than previous generations. Or if they are better able to make decisions on our behalf. Read on and judge for yourself. The point is that politicians, who actually vote on their own salary increases (can you say "conflict of interest"?), were encouraged to raise their own salaries and the benefits that went with them. The best benefit they could give themselves was a fantastic pension plan that rewarded them with a lifetime of income for what often turned out to be a very short period of actual work.

When Losers Become Winners

The 2011 federal election demonstrates this plan in action. The 113 defeated and/or retiring members of parliament (MPs) will collectively receive $4.9 million[1] in pensions their first year under a plan—for those 113 members alone—that will eventually cost taxpayers $1.1 billion, based on a life expectancy of 85 years. Seventeen former MPs qualify for more than $100,000 per year, including former Bloc Québécois leader Gilles Duceppe, who receives $141,000 annually for his years of effort in trying to break up the country. *Vive le Québec libre*! As an elected representative paid by taxpaying Canadians, Duceppe would have received his pension—from those same Canadians—even if he had succeeded in his attempts at secession and become the prime minister of an independent Québec!

MP pensions are paid starting at age 55, so those retiring closest to that age receive pensions for the longest period. Five MPs will receive more than $3 million each thanks to their early retirement age.[2] Even those MPs who did not serve the minimum six years to qualify for a pension will receive a severance payment equal to 50 per cent of their annual salary. For deposed Liberal leader Michael Ignatieff, this severance was $116,000.[3]

The biggest loser in this scenario was Labrador MP Todd Russell, defeated after serving five years and 11 months—one month short of pension eligibility. The Canadian Taxpayers Federation estimates[4] that this will save taxpayers $600,000—unless Russell wins again in the next election. He certainly has incentive.

Once the trend of awarding themselves pay raises, great pensions, benefits, and severance was established, it became increasingly difficult for politicians to turn down the ever-increasing salary and pension requests of all the government workers in their domain. And whenever a ruling political party tried to limit these increases, employees threatened massive strikes and disruption of public services. In many cases these strikes became reality, and in every case, politicians eventually backed down.

Debt vs. Deficit

If the government spends more than it collects in a year, the shortfall is called an operating deficit, or simply the deficit. The deficit is the cost of providing a year's worth of services to Canadians, minus revenue taken in that year from taxes. Services such as health care, education, and road work that most Canadians say are insufficient anyway.

The debt on the other hand, is the accumulation of yearly deficits. Most people are confused about these two terms, largely because the media and politicians focus on the deficit—which is current news—and ignore the debt. Part of any yearly deficit includes interest payments on the debt. However there is an elephant in the room that promises to be much more damaging to your future than simply the yearly deficit, interest payments, and accumulated debt that will need to be repaid, hopefully before you die. This elephant is federal, provincial, and municipal government pension obligations, and is more damaging because this cost provides no real value to the taxpayer. In fact, whenever a public sector employee retires, two costs are incurred—the retiree's pension, plus the cost of the worker hired to replace him. With life expectancy now at 85 and the average retirement age of our public sector at 59 and dropping, pension costs will become astronomical. As you can see in the example of our retiring politicians, paying for just 113 of them incurs a bill of $1.1 billion. What will be the final cost when our 3,500,000-plus current public sector workers (federal, provincial and municipal) are retired?

Let's set aside the rhetoric for a minute and look at the amount of your money already siphoned off to fund these ever-increasing employment and pension benefits, and how their associated costs have been accumulating. Our federal government has approximately 420,000[5] employees with a basic pension plan that guarantees them up to 70 per cent of their final five years' average income for life and/or the life of their spouse if their spouse outlives them. What this guarantee means is that if their Canada Pension Plan income is less than 70 per cent of their last five years' average annual working income (which is virtually guaranteed, given their high incomes), and their employee pension plan is underfunded and can't pay this amount (most of them are), the government will top this up with additional funds from taxes—and these pension commitments legally come before all other government expenditures. In fact, in 2009 the C.D. Howe Institute, a leading Canadian think tank started in 1958 to "research and promote educational issues related to public economic policy," calculated that the pension plan for federal employees alone is short about $200 billion.[6] This is impossible to pay under our current system. The entire yearly revenue for the federal government in 2010 was only $231 billion—and the government spent $280 billion without touching this pension shortfall.

Nowhere is this shortage more apparent than in the federal politicians' own pension fund. According to the pension fund's annual report to Parliament for 2008–09[7] the fund for members of Parliament rose by 10 per cent during the 2008/09 global recession. How did they achieve this miracle of growth in an economy in which private pension plans lost 21 per cent of their value, and even the staid Canada Pension Plan (CPP) lost 14 per cent? Easy—there is no actual money in the fund, it's simply a guarantee that politicians will receive a specific pension. This guarantee currently sits at more than $500 million and has an interest set by regulation and guaranteed by taxpayers. So while your RRSP may be at risk from market fluctuations, you can be comforted by the fact that your elected representatives have no risk—just like your other 420,000 employees. "Not a dollar of real cash has gone into these (politicians') plans," said Bill Robson, president of the C.D. Howe Institute, a conservative think tank, "so when the time comes to pay the pensions, all of this money is going to have to be raised either by real borrowing—like actually floating bonds that people pay cash to invest in—or through taxes."

Canadian Taxpayers Federation federal director Kevin Gaudet said he doubts many Canadians are aware that "not only do they not have enough of their own money saved, but they're also paying through the nose in their taxes so that they can feather the retirement beds of public sector employees and politicians. I think they ought to be mad. It's a huge discrepancy."

The taxpayer's federation calculates that after serving only six years, an MP is entitled to an annual pension of $27,000. Long-serving MPs can collect more than $100,000 a year. Having just completed his fourth year as prime minister (2011), Stephen Harper is now eligible to collect a special retirement allowance once he turns 65—on top of his MP's pension, which he can begin collecting at 55. By Gaudet's calculation, that means Harper will eventually collect an annual pension and allowance worth at least $178,000.

If you are a government worker, this apparently just looks like a fair deal. After all, Canada's moral standard for taking care of its seniors is that we respect their contribution to our country and want them to be comfortable in their old age. We already have a health care system that provides more benefits to seniors than any other age group. Again, going back 30 years or so, the general idea was that people working for big business, such as the automobile industry, the steel industry, and other manufacturers that built our country, had strong unions which had negotiated better wages, benefits, and pensions for their workers. Better, that is, than the compensation packages offered to public sector workers. Public service unionized employees were simply trying to keep pace. However something completely unforeseen has taken place and the pendulum has swung in the other direction. Private industry in Canada has been decimated by global forces, resulting in massive layoffs, plant closures, and entire industries being moved to foreign countries—resulting in a significant erosion in incomes and benefits. Private company pensions in particular have been hard hit, in part because government regulations that were meant to ensure future pension payments were lenient at best, and non-existent at worst.

Why are Pensions the Problem?

Pensions. Pension debate. Pension reform. The mere words put most of us to sleep and yet at some point in your life, the quality of your pension will become the very foundation of the quality of your life. It has been said that the only two things you can count on in life are death and taxes, but in Canada it may be more accurate to say death, taxes, and pensions, because virtually everyone in Canada is guaranteed some form of pension income once they reach a certain age or become disabled and cannot work.

"Okay, okay," we can hear you saying. "I get that pensions are important, but what do government employee pensions have to do with me?" Well, it turns out that most of the money that politicians have borrowed in your name over the past 30 years has accumulated in pension plans[8] for a select group of people—your employees. Don't think you have employees? Think again. In a government "of the people, for the people, by the people" as democracy is often described, all government employees are actually employees of the people. That would be you. The same can be said of your elected officials, who secure their jobs by way of winning more votes than the other "job applicants" who run in elections.

It's very easy for individuals to completely lose their connection with our democratic system, our elected officials, and our government employees when they become disconnected from the reality of where the money comes from to fund all of these jobs and the programs they are associated with. We'll deal with this in detail in Chapter 8, but we think it's important that you understand that *you* are the employer of all of these people since you actually pay their salaries, benefits, and most importantly—their pensions.

So now that you understand that you are the employer in this circumstance and that all the money for the system comes out of your pocket by way of taxes, let's consider the suggestion that most of the

FIGURE 1.1: Total Retirement Assets of Canadians (1990-2007)

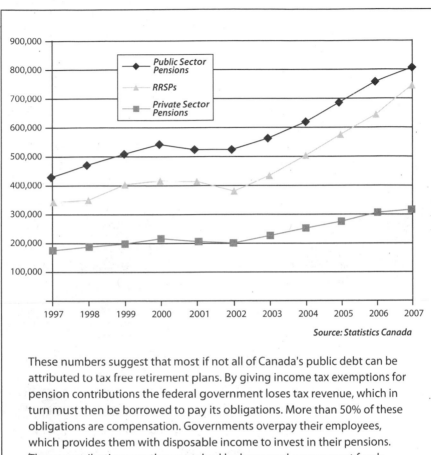

Source: Statistics Canada

These numbers suggest that most if not all of Canada's public debt can be attributed to tax free retirement plans. By giving income tax exemptions for pension contributions the federal government loses tax revenue, which in turn must then be borrowed to pay its obligations. More than 50% of these obligations are compensation. Governments overpay their employees, which provides them with disposable income to invest in their pensions. These contributions are then matched by borrowed government funds, and when the pension funds are in deficit, governments borrow again to top them up.

money that has been borrowed in your name by our various levels of government has been funneled into pensions for your employees. Keep in mind that this borrowing is an ongoing process with no end in sight unless we see some very dramatic changes in the way government business is conducted.

So here are the numbers Canada's total provincial and gross federal debt is somewhere in the range of $1.27 trillion,⁹ and increasing daily. The total current assets of all government employee pension funds is in the range of $800 billion. If you can take a step away from the rhetoric of who contributed how much to what, it's pretty easy to connect those two dots and conclude that a large part of our debt has been created by governments borrowing money to fund the pensions of public sector workers.

> Few Californians in the private sector have $1 million in savings, but that's effectively the retirement account they guarantee to public employees who opt to retire at age 55 and are entitled to monthly, inflation-protected checks of $3,000 for the rest of their lives . . . legislators don't want a government of the people, by the people, and for the people, but a government of the employees, by the employees, and for the employees.
>
> Arnold Schwarzenegger, (Governor of California), "Public Pensions and Our Fiscal Future." Wall Street Journal, August 27, 2010.

This $800 million has already been transferred from your pocket to theirs, but your total debt obligation doesn't stop with the money that's already been transferred. Because public sector pension payouts are guaranteed by taxpayers, you have, in effect, signed promissory notes—by proxy of course, since you weren't directly consulted on any of these decisions—that commit you to hundreds of billions of dollars in future payments. That's right: most of these pension funds are "underfunded." This means that the $800 million that the funds already have in their coffers is far short of being enough money to pay the pensions that politicians have agreed to on your behalf. And by "far short," we mean that these lucrative public sector pension plans are currently estimated by us to be underfunded in excess of $300 billion dollars. The pension guarantees are based on unrealistic expectations of strong economic growth and consistently high investment returns for years to come—windfalls we haven't seen in Canada for the past 10 years. We expect the shortfall will be much larger than this. The actual cost will be guaranteed by you the taxpayer, regardless of investment return. So even if the markets remain stagnant, as they have for the past 10 years, you will pay the full pension amount to your retired employees.

It's not uncommon for average taxpayers to become incensed when they realize that for the past 30 years,[10] as they have struggled to support their families in the face of an ever-increasing tax burden, the taxes they pay have been siphoned off to provide ever-increasing salaries and benefits for public sector employees and politicians. Supporting these pacts has already cost us $1.2 trillion in government debt. Every man, woman, and child in Canada now owes $35,000 worth of this government debt,[11] and we must pay it back, with interest! Add in the $300 billion pension funding liability, and the many other "hidden" debts at the municipal level, in the form of other post-employment benefits (OPEBs) (which we will talk about later), and you can see why pundits refer to a "pension tsunami."

The Wage Gap—Skyrocketing Compensation Packages

So, public sector employees have better pension plans than most Canadians, but do public service workers really make more money than private sector employees? This has been a recent debate as unions defend their territory. Let's look at the studies. The Canadian Federation of Independent Business put together a comprehensive analysis called *Wage Watch*,[12] which highlights the gap in wages between private sector workers and the civil service. The report, released in 2008, concludes the following:

Detailed analysis of 2006 census findings on full-time earnings by sector and occupation shows that government and public sector employees are paid roughly 8–17 per cent more than similarly employed individuals in the private sector. In addition, taking into account significantly higher paid benefits and shorter workweeks, the public sector total compensation advantage balloons past 30 per cent. Expressed in dollar terms, public sector employers have a combined wage and benefits bill that is $19 billion higher annually than if they had kept costs to private sector norms.

This $19 billion includes wages, benefits, and pensions. Another report recently released by the Frontier Centre for Public Policy, a Winnipeg-based think tank updated the annual cost of just the wages paid to the public sector as $2.6 billion per year more than equivalent private sector wages.[13] This $16.4 billion difference shows the true cost of the "add-on benefits" that the public sector has negotiated for itself at taxpayer expense. Most Canadians are not aware of the existence or cost of these benefits because they are not reported as part of wage settlements or given a dollar value in media reports. Add-ons include contributions made by the government to employee pension plans and various benefits programs including dental, health, life insurance, and sick pay. The public hears about a 3 per cent wage increase for instance, but not about the corresponding cost of benefits or the future cost of higher pension guarantees based on the higher wages.

Beyond simple wages, there is a multiplier effect on pensions for every dollar wage increase given to an employee. As wages go up so too do other post-employee benefits (OPEB) costs, such as health insurance, dental insurance, life insurance, sick pay, holiday pay, and unfunded pension liabilities, which are based on retirement salary. These associated costs have become a huge and unrecognized burden hidden in the back pages of the financial statements of your local hospital, school board, municipality or university.

While many public sector employees retire early their contracts entitle them to continue to receive paid health care benefits until age 65. Taxpayers pick up this employee benefits tab for early retired workers. These costs are reported as future employee benefit liabilities or debts; in effect, this is like a loan to early retirees that is paid back by all taxpayers through future taxes. Health care rates are rising by 8–10 per cent a year and these costs add up. For every dollar of wage increase, the pension fund requires $16 in contributions to cover associated retirement benefits. So a reported $1,500 wage increase for an employee means that the pension plan will need an additional $24,000 by the time the employee retires. Of course the employee will never contribute that much, so the government reports it as an OPEB or future employee benefit liability.

At the City of Toronto in 2009, for example, OPEBs were $2.6 billion.[14] Ontario's Hydro One[15] had $980 million of OPEB liability on its books, as do many other government entities. You can guess what this will do to your tax rates and your Hydro bill.

At the other end of the equation, benefits paid out continue to outpace contributions paid into these public sector pension funds. This discrepancy will eventually be made up by taxpayers and is added to the pension deficit or shortfall. Demographic and investment trends indicate that this gap will widen every year for the next 20 years as baby boomers retire and live longer than any previous generation, and stock markets suffer from continual RRSP withdrawals. Currently, Ontario Teachers' Pension Plan (OTPP) annual benefit payments exceed $4 billion while annual contributions are only $2.2 billion. This trend will continue and accelerate in the future.

The report by the Frontier Centre for Public Policy we mentioned earlier found that:

- Federal government public administration workers saw their average wage increase by 59 per cent between 1998 and 2009. This is almost twice the rate of wage growth in the economy as a whole, which grew at approximately 30 per cent. Provincial administration came in second at 55 per cent, and municipal increases were close to the national average at 33 per cent.

FIGURE 1.2 Provincial Government "Pay Premium" (2008)

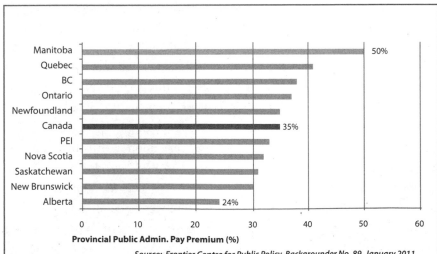

Source: *Frontier Centre for Public Policy, Backgrounder No. 89, January 2011*

Provincial and Federal public sector compensation packages have consistently surpassed those in corresponding private sector employment. Whereas once public sector workers were offered good pensions to offset lower wages, today our civil service is paid more both during their working years and after retirement. Plus they retire earlier than private sector workers.

- No other major industry tracked by Statistics Canada experienced wage growth that was close to that seen in the public administration category. The next highest rates were in the real estate, mining, and oil extraction industries at 46 per cent. Others included waste management at 35 per cent, construction at 34 per cent, finance, insurance, and business management at 33 per cent, and food services at 31 per cent.
- At the bottom of the list were manufacturing at 19 per cent, retail at 17 per cent, and forestry at 11 per cent.
- Rapid public administration wage growth has caused the pay gap between the average public servant and the average worker in the economy to widen considerably. In 1998, the average annual wage for federal public administration workers was approximately $10,000 higher than the average worker in the economy. By 2009, that gap had grown to $25,000.[16]

It's interesting that we have a constant focus on wage disparity by gender, age, and ethnicity, but any focus on "sector discrimination" between public and private sector workers is attacked as unfair by public sector unions.

Let's go back to our discussion of fair wages and pension funding. If the government pays a building inspector $5,000 a year more than you can afford (meaning that the government borrows the money and adds it to the yearly deficit and accumulated debt), and that inspector puts this $5,000 into his union-managed pension fund and that $5,000 is matched by his employer (the taxpayer again), we can say that his pension fund has been totally funded by taxpayers. Of the $1.05 trillion in private and public trusteed pension funds (not including private RRSP funds), $800 billion has been funded by taxpayers on behalf of public sector employees in this way.[17] The remaining is in private sector employee pension plans.

It's funny to hear people comparing government jobs to private sector positions and claiming these jobs are in some way the same. In private business the perpetrators of this pension Ponzi scheme would have been behind bars years ago. In government we re-elect them, overpay them, give them tenure and huge payouts if they get caught being incompetent or unethical and have to step down before their terms expire; or great pensions if they can outlast the chase. Does this sound fair to you?

Staff costs—including salaries, benefits, and pensions (all known as compensation costs)—are the biggest costs of government. These range from a low of 45–50 per cent at the municipal level to as high as 80–90 per cent for police and education budgets. Here are some recent examples:

% Spending on Salaries and Benefits

	Revenue	Salaries	Benefits	Total	%
Vancouver School Board 2010	$ 560,473	$374,915	$ 91,664	$466,579	83.25%
University of Calgary 2010	$1,034,130	$502,482	$101,957	$604,439	58.45%
City of Winnipeg 2008	$1,144,074	$539,405	INC	$539,405	47.15%
Hamilton Health Sciences 2010	$1,214,444	$722,952	INC	$722,952	59.53%

The question of fairness comes down to who is paying the bill. If the private sector can run a profitable business and reward its employees with higher salaries, more benefits, shorter careers, and higher pensions, more power to it. Our governments will then also receive higher income by way of income tax on workers' salaries, taxes on corporate profits, and so on, as part of the redistribution of wealth. But if our governments are borrowing money every year—money that taxpayers will have to pay back—in order to provide the best salaries, benefits, and pensions for public sector employees, is this defensible? We think not.

Reduced Workload

But wait, it gets even better. The next step in the master plan to create a better life for Canadians (which we believe is the purpose of government, is it not?) was to systematically reduce the workload on government employees. This began by shortening the work week for government employees, now typically 35 hours per week, down from an average of 40 hours a week 30 years ago. Next we saw an increase in vacation time, to up to eight months a year for senior employees. And lastly, just to be done with the whole bother of working altogether, we saw a reduction of years on the job necessary for workers to earn their pensions. Before we go into that, however, a word on the "age of retirement."

If you ask Canadians what the age of retirement is, or if you look on any global information site that compares Canada to other countries, you will find that the age of retirement in Canada is referenced to eligibility for the Canada Pension Plan (CPP) or the equivalent Québec Pension Plan (QPP) which replaces the CPP in Québec. This age is currently 65. "Early retirement" is an option at age 60, with reduced CPP benefits, and no Old Age Security (OAS) or Guaranteed Income Supplement (GIS), two additional federally-funded pensions that are not available until age 65. The CPP is the government-managed plan for all working Canadians into which employers and employees have been paying since 1966. If you have paid into the CPP, you are entitled to receive full benefits—based on your employment contributions—at 65 or a reduced monthly payment at age 60. This typically means working 40 years or more, and is often referred to as the "40-year plan."

Public sector employees, however—the ones whose salaries you pay— have been able to whittle that down to just 35 years, and in the case of some specific jobs, such as those in the police force, fire department, or military, just 30 years of service are required before employees can retire. In fact, the average retirement age in the public sector is now 59[18] with many thousands of civil servants retiring closer to 50. Of course, they don't receive those pensions until they're 65, right? Wrong. While the rest of Canada's taxpayers must wait until at least age 60 to receive a reduced pension from CPP/QPP, and age 65 for a full pension, government employees begin receiving CPP immediately upon retirement. This CPP equivalent is known as a bridge benefit because it "bridges" the time from early retirement until age 65. This benefit is topped up from the employee pension fund to make the full pension amount. The bridge benefit stops when the employee becomes entitled to CPP/QPP benefits.[19] This effectively gives the public servant CPP from the first day of retirement.

Seems that the public sector took to heart insurance company London Life's concept of "Freedom 55" as an achievable goal for themselves. Most Canadians will never achieve this level of financial freedom at any age.

Having reached only the age of 50–59, public servants don't have to retire. They can continue to work at those same positions until they reach 65, and many do, "retiring" one day and then returning to work shortly thereafter. Sometimes they return to the same job but usually another government job, because of the connections they have within the system. The only difference is that they are now collecting both the pension and a regular paycheque. This is known as "double dipping." Plus, these workers begin building a second pension. If they are able to work another 15 years in their new job, they will qualify for almost half the value of a full second pension (equal to 30 per cent of income), which can put them up to 100 per cent of their previous working income in total.[20] So few of these people actually retire the first time—what they are really doing is retiring from that particular job. Many of them get another job in the public sector. Retire twice and get two pensions? Sign us up for that!

Double Dipping

In Newfoundland the provincial auditor discovered that during 2010 a group of 443 retired teachers earned $15.6 million in pensions and $5.2 million in wages.

CBC News, January 26, 2011

We often read reports of top civil servants, such as police chiefs,[21] fire chiefs, government department heads, and others in senior public sector positions, retiring in their early 50s and listing "personal reasons" as their motivation for leaving highly-rewarding jobs. None of them ever seem to say, "I qualify for 70 per cent of my income as pension now, so it makes no sense to continue working." Strangely though, these personal reasons always seem to crop up at the 30- or 35-year mark, just as their pensions become available. The public statements of retiring senior civil servants are carefully crafted to avoid any hint of the financial bonanza that awaits them, so the public never learns the truth. Perhaps if every 50-something public sector retiree said, "I'm retiring because I have a full pension now, and I'm going to spend the rest of my life playing golf while you pay me," or "I can get 70 per cent of my salary for doing nothing, so I'm going to take that, and then go out and get another job working for the government and get 100 per cent of that, plus build a second pension for when I really retire," the taxpaying public would know where its tax dollars are actually going.

So there you have it. The people you chose to govern on your behalf have systematically borrowed and/or obligated you to the tune of an estimated $1.2 trillion to make sure that your employees have the best of all possible worlds.

Living Under the Bell Jar

The fundamental purpose of our government is to provide common services to protect and enhance the lives of all Canadians. Essential services such as defence, police, and capital projects in the domain of public works have long been provided through government taxation. Provision of nonessential services—ones that could be provided privately or by volunteers, such as fire fighting, health care, education, libraries, culture and sports, garbage collection, and maintenance of public works—is a sign of a modern, more controlling government, and Canadians have come to expect these types of services to be provided by the government. Many political commentators refer to this level of government intervention in our daily lives as living in a nanny state.

These services have been funded by Canada's progressive tax model, under which income tax rates increase along with a person's taxable income. The intent is to have those who can afford to pay more provide a larger contribution to the public good. A balancing act is required to provide services, while at the same time maintaining incentives to motivate and reward people for working hard to get ahead, thereby increasing their own incomes and generating higher tax revenues for the government.

Under our current system, income taxes alone are not sufficient to cover government expenditures, and rather than increase the taxes paid by the wealthy and corporations our governments have created an array of consumption taxes. These include the now-defunct Federal Sales Tax, the Provincial Sales Tax (PST) in most provinces, and the Goods and Services Tax (GST), now combined in some provinces as the Harmonized Sales Tax (HST), in addition to specific additional taxes on gasoline, entertainment, alcohol, and other items. These taxes are not considered progressive since they cost lower income earners a larger percentage of their income than they do higher income earners. For instance, two people earning vastly different incomes would pay the same amount of tax on a tank of gas.

Naturally, managing these billions of dollars of ever-expanding services and the labyrinthian system which collects these taxes requires the hiring of more civil servants with their inflated salaries, luxurious benefits packages, and eventually unsustainable pensions, driving yearly deficits and long-term debt ever higher.

Note that while the private sector reeled from a collapsing global economy in 2008 and 2009, the growth of the public sector continued unabated. The expansion of the federal civil service as an example, in the five years of Stephen Harper's rule so far, is nothing short of stunning. And the corresponding increase in public sector wage, benefits, and pension settlements has grown hand-in-hand with the deficit.

Had we built this country and provided these services with cash flow generated by a thriving economy and an efficient tax-based government we could all be rightfully proud. Unfortunately we have built this country by mortgaging our future, and the mortgage renewal date is coming soon.

The bell jar is a system that protects and isolates a developing country's tiny class of elites. These elites are shielded by laws and customs from having to compete with the majority in their society.

Hernando De Soto[22]

The bell jar concept can be used to describe all societies wherein a "protected class" lives within the bell jar and a "vulnerable class" lives outside. The guiding principle behind democracy and Canada's Charter of Rights and Freedoms is to include all Canadians within the bell jar. Certainly when it comes to access to and protection under the legal system, the opportunities of higher education, gender and ethnic equality rights, and freedom of speech and religion, Canada is inclusive. However, when it comes to economic principles within our society, many of us are stuck on the outside of the bell jar.

FIGURE 1.3 Canada's Growing Civil Service

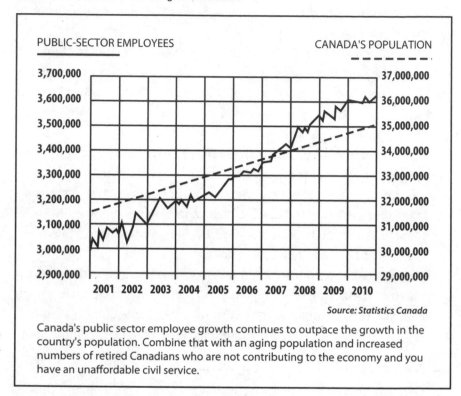

PUBLIC-SECTOR EMPLOYEES   CANADA'S POPULATION

Source: Statistics Canada

Canada's public sector employee growth continues to outpace the growth in the country's population. Combine that with an aging population and increased numbers of retired Canadians who are not contributing to the economy and you have an unaffordable civil service.

As we will see during a closer examination of the disparity between the salaries, benefits, and pensions of private and public sector workers, public sector unions have successfully insulated their members within a bell jar which excludes non-member taxpayers. More specifically, these unions have engineered a redistribution of wealth from all levels of society into the bank and pension accounts of their members.

2

THE DEVIL IS IN THE DETAILS

If you are not a public servant, the odds are very good that you will not have a genuine pension in retirement. Now, public sector workers may say, "We paid for our pension coverage!" but the reality is that as a taxpayer, so did you; except you will not see any benefit from your contributions. In addition, defined benefit pensions in the public sector are the only pensions that come with a government guarantee.
Moshe A. Milevsky and Alexandra C. Macqueen,
Pensionize Your Nest Egg

Let's consider how pensions are created. Step out of the box for a minute and ask, "Why are pensions based on what you did when you were working, since the whole point of a pension is to provide income for you when you are no longer working?" Let us explain.

Take the case of a chief of police, police officer, and police secretary. Among other factors, the responsibilities and skills entailed by each job are different, and are therefore accorded different salaries. We could argue about the relative value of these workers to society and the fairness of their income, but once they are retired they are all of equal value to society. Why should their pension be based on what they earned while they were working? Take a look at the numbers.

A police chief in a medium-sized city might earn $150,000 annually. A police officer might reach $100,000 a year, while a secretary earns

$50,000 annually. Could the police force operate effectively without all three? Probably not, however their respective pay is reflective of a number of considerations including training, risk, responsibility, and other factors such as replacement cost. It is likely easier to replace the secretary than it is the police officer. The chief's position requires leadership in addition to public relations and political savvy, and in our society these skills are more highly rewarded than those of the officer.

These career income differences have evolved through years of evaluation, negotiation, and experience. But once these three individuals retire, these values become moot. The police chief with his $100,000 pension might easily retire to Florida. The police officer with his $70,000 pension might contribute his time to minor sports organizations. The secretary with her $35,000 pension might volunteer at the local food bank and spearhead fundraising efforts for years to come. It could be that in retirement, the value that these individuals contribute to our country is inverse to what they contributed during their working lives. So why are their pensions based on their previously-earned incomes?

Naturally the police chief, with a lifetime of higher earnings could more easily have contributed to his RRSP, would have been able to afford a more luxurious house and lifestyle, and would have a more secure retirement anyway, so why does he need a higher pension than the secretary? We ask this in the context that you are paying for their pensions as their employer, so you should decide if this is fair value for your tax dollar.

The truth is that these pensions have no relation to retirement but are, in actual fact, deferred income. This is significant when one considers the overall wage and benefits packages of public sector employee that unions have negotiated over the past 30 years. When you include the deferred income portion of these contracts you see the real size of the windfall. As we saw in the Frontier Centre report, wages and benefits for the public sector have wildly outpaced those of industry, but the difference in pension outcomes dwarfs even those figures. These lifetime pensions based on the highest three or five years of income enshrine the inequality of the system until death. By spreading out the total compensation that government workers receive by hiding it as a pension (when, in fact, it is deferred income), the public sector is able to conceal these excessive compensation packages from view—and from taxes. This loss of income tax revenue also contributes to our deficit. Recent tax changes allow married pensioners to split their pension incomes, which may significantly lower the total combined income tax paid, and takes this tax avoidance to a new level.

Funding Retirements

To understand how pension inequality, called pension apartheid by some, will affect you, it is important to have a basic understanding of how pensions are structured and how Canadians can go about funding their retirements. (We'll try to make this part short so you don't fall asleep, but it is important information.) All working Canadians will receive pension income from the Canada and/or Québec Pension Plan (CPP/QPP) once they reach the age of 65 (reduced benefits are available at age 60). The CPP has achieved its minimalist goal—to provide retired Canadians with a pension of up to 25 per cent of the average Canadian income[1]—but has also created a false sense of security for Canadians. Unless they care for a senior and understand his finances, young adults generally have no idea how much their CPP will pay on retirement and typically don't inquire until their late 50s. They work for 40 years under the assumption that their CPP will be adequate to support them financially during retirement. By the time they understand the reality, it is generally too late to create a significant supplement to what most will see as a meagre CPP payment. The average annual CPP payment in 2011 was $6,144, while the maximum payment was $11,520.[2] Contrast this with the average new police pension (for those retiring in 2011) from the City of Montreal of $59,000 per year (at age 53).[3] Indexed for inflation, an average (or even maximum) CPP payout won't come close to supporting most Canadian retirees in the lifestyle to which they have become accustomed.

We urge all Canadians to get a periodic update of their Canada Pension Plan Statement of Contributions. This is a statement of your CPP account with the government and is easily accessible online at Service Canada.[4] It will show you how much you would receive upon retirement. You want to be able to accurately estimate how much the CPP pensions will add to your retirement program.

The CPP is considered a defined benefit (DB) pension fund, meaning that specific payments are guaranteed regardless of whether the fund has enough money. These benefits are not, however, guaranteed by contractual law as are public sector pensions, and can be adjusted up or down by parliament, depending on the strength of the economy. Equivalent pensions in Greece and the UK for instance, have been cut as part of austerity measures. (On the other hand, the federal Conservatives recently increased the Old Age Security (OAS) segment of the national pension plan.) Shortfalls in the CPP must be made up from taxes. The fund is held in various investments including stocks. The CPP has $56 billion in equity investments, with 66 per cent ($37 billion) in foreign companies. This makes it very vulnerable to market fluctuations. As of the end of 2010, the plan required $1.9 trillion in assets to meet future pension obligations, and by 2019 the total actuarial liability of the CPP is expected to be $2.8 trillion. Remember, the fund had $153.2 billion at the end of 2010.[5] And just as with public sector pensions, taxpayers are on the hook for any CPP-related underfunding.

Some of the assumptions on which the CPP system is based have to be very accurate in order to prevent a future time bomb. Any fluctuations in any one of these assumptions can upset the apple cart. The key assumptions are based on life expectancy, the size of the workforce, future immigration trends, wage levels, rates of return on investments, and total future contributions into the plan. Based on the assumptions we have used for various other workplace pensions, and the shortfalls and risks they have created, Canadians should be very concerned about the performance of the CPP. The plan's projections are based on a consistent return of 6 per cent per year in perpetuity. If this is not achieved, the difference will have to come from general revenues, which in turn means less money for education, health care, and other public services.

The 10-year S&P/TSX Composite index average rate of return to the middle of 2010 was only about 8 per cent[6]—in total—for the entire 10-year period. The CPP's annual 6 per cent projection may turn out to be wildly optimistic. The University of British Columbia (UBC) Staff Pension Plan, for instance, returned an average of only 3.79 per cent from 2001 to 2010.[7] It is possible we may see performance in the markets similar to Japan's because of our demographics. Japan has very similar demographics to Canada but is about 10 years more advanced in its aging cycle. As the percentage of retired people increases, national economic productivity drops, leading to stagnation and lower investment returns. International companies may choose to build new plants in countries with a younger workforce, which offers longer (and usually cheaper) productivity, reduced health costs and delayed pension liabilities. Japan's stock market since the market highs of the '90s has lost 75 per cent of its value.[8] Canadian pension funds are counting on positive returns every year to fund their future commitments. A long period of underperforming stock markets would be catastrophic.

The CPP is set up so that it is funded with matching contributions from both employer and employee. Currently these contributions are 4.95 per cent of salary up to a maximum eligible income ceiling called the Yearly Maximum Pensionable Earnings (YMPE). A self-employed person contributes both the employer and employee portions and pays 9.9 per cent of total earnings. In 2011, the YMPE was set at $48,300, so the maximum contribution was $4,781. It's interesting to note that when the CPP was created in 1965, average life expectancy was only 67, so the plan was expected to fund a two-year retirement, whereas today, with life expectancies in the mid 80s, the CPP has been widely recognized by just about everyone as being inadequate. Realistically, any demographer over the past 20 years would have identified the CPP as insufficient (and many have), but it is only in the last few years, as the baby boomers retire en masse, that the government is being forced to focus on the problems that our false expectations have created.

Unions and some pension pundits are suggesting increases in CPP benefit rates to increase the national pension available to Canadians. A rate hike would require additional contributions by workers and employers into the plan. The current government has opted for the creation of the optional Pooled Registered Pension Plan[9] (PRPP) which will be a second workplace plan for all Canadian workers, but how much more can you realistically take away from your own family needs to pay into all of these liability pools for retired people?

In addition to CPP, Canadians can use Registered Retirement Savings Plans (RRSPs) to provide themselves with retirement income. A recent addition to savings options was introduced with the Tax Free Savings Account (TFSA). If you have started your own retirement savings plan—either an

RRSP or a TFSA—you will know that the basic concept is that you put money away every year while you're working to create a nest egg you can draw on in your retirement years. You can invest your money in any number of options, including equities (stocks), mutual funds, Exchange Traded Funds (ETFs), Guaranteed Investment Certificates, and the like, and hope that the markets are good to you. Neither the RRSP nor the TFSA is actually a pension, but rather a savings vehicle that the government hopes you will have when you retire. Since neither is a pension, money can be withdrawn at any time, and in fact, many RRSPs have been dissolved or reduced by their owners in the face of economic hardships over the past decade, or have been used as down payments by first-time home buyers who aren't earning enough money to fund their house purchase the traditional way.

Unfortunately, the RRSP program has been a spectacular failure in Canada. StatsCan states that fewer than 6.2 million tax filers contributed to RRSPs in 2008, and that the median balance of RRSPs in 2005 was only $25,000.[10] When you consider that the maximum amount of income that you can shelter each year in an RRSP (as of 2011) is $22,450 (based on a maximum of 18 per cent of your income), and that the average Canadian income is only $41,000, it's clear that the RRSP program has proven to be of little value in providing significant pension security for the average Canadian. In addition, the loss of income tax revenue from these sheltered incomes has contributed to our national debt.

Employee Pension Plans Explained

Employee pension plans are managed by employers, unions, governments, and in some cases, such as the large provincial public sector plans, independently managed by professional pension fund managers. These pension funds are created from money contributed through payroll deductions. Employees contribute a percentage of their wages and, generally speaking, employers match these contributions. Private sector employers and municipal and provincial governments usually match contributions dollar for dollar. The federal government goes one better and contributes roughly $2.34 for every $1 the employee contributes.

There are two types of pensions: defined contribution (DC) and defined benefit (DB). Under a DC plan, the employee and the company each contribute a specific or "defined" amount of money to the pension plan, and the pension payment in retirement is based on how well the investment of the pension fund has fared. Most private companies have switched to DC plans because these plans are not required to guarantee benefit amounts. As long as contributions are being made, there is no possibility of a pension fund deficit, or unfunded liability.

DB plans guarantee the amount of income a pensioner receives from the pension during retirement (the "benefit"), regardless of the success or failure of the fund's investments. Benefits are based on a variety of factors, including salary, age, and years of service. Generally speaking, they are calculated on the number of years worked multiplied by a number known as the pension accrual rate. Eighty per cent of public sector employees have DB pensions, and not only do these public sector plans guarantee a fixed-rate of income, they also guarantee an upward adjustment of that income to keep pace with inflation, so public sector workers' pensions never lose their buying power.

Most public sector unions use an accrual rate of 2 per cent, which means that you multiply the number of years you have worked times two to find your pension multiplier. Then multiply your earnings by this number. Public sector pensions guarantee to replace 70 per cent of income once they are fully qualified, which means that after 35 years ($2\% \times 35 = 70\%$) the pension is maximized.

Public sector pensions are usually based on the final three or five years of salary or the highest earning years, while private section pensions are based on average income over an entire career. The examples below show how this one small difference in terms can make a huge difference in benefits.

Example—Public Sector Final Salary Calculation

Pension based on $90,000 income for a qualified worker with 35 years of service.

Last 5 years' income: $90,000/year
Calculation: 35 years $\times$ 2% = 70%
Annual Pension: $90,000 $\times$ 70% = $ 63,000/year

Example—Private Sector Career Average Calculation

Pension based on $90,000 income for a qualified worker with 35 years of service.

Average 35 years' income: $60,000/year
Calculation: 35 years × 2% = 70%
Annual Pension: $60,000 × 70% = $ 42,000/year[11]

Note that public safety workers, such as police, firefighters, and members of the military are eligible for a full pension after 30 years of service. Their calculation is based on an accrual rate of 2.33 per cent.

The gap between public and private sector pensions is widening every year. The percentage of public sector employees covered in DB plans remains the same, even as employment levels increase, while private sector pensions are being converted to DC plans and their coverage is rapidly falling. The year 2009 was a landmark for pensions in Canada. For the first time, there were more public sector employees with pensions than private sector employees. In that year, 3,026,400 public employees had pensions, an increase of 2.6 per cent from the previous year, while only 2,997,300 private sector employees were covered, a drop of 2.1 per cent. The trend has continued and the gap is even wider now.[12]

Supplementary Supersize-me Pensions

As if these indexed, guaranteed pensions weren't enough, there is an ever-growing number of your senior public sector employees, such as municipal department heads, university professors, and health care administrators, who are paid salaries beyond the legal pensionable limits. The Income Tax Act limited the qualifying annual pensionable income in 2008 to a maximum of $131,000. At a top rate of 70 per cent of income, this limits the pensions you are guaranteeing to a maximum of $91,700, including CPP. This should be more than enough for a person to retire on, but wily employees and politicians who were paid more than $131,000 felt they were being short-changed. Using a creativity they can never seem to find to stay within their budgets, but can always muster up for their own gain, they came up with a plan to create a new fund called the Supplementary Employee Retirement Plan (SERP).[13] Naturally, these very highly-paid employees contribute only a small portion of the total cost of these plans. StatsCan shows that these plans have accumulated $199 billion[14] to pay the pensions of these super-sized pensions. In actual fact, taxpayers have paid more into these plans for the select few ($199 billion) than they have contributed to the CPP plan ($153 billion) for the other 18,000,000 working stiffs.[15]

It's interesting that when it comes to the private sector, the pensionable income limit for CPP contributions is only $48,300 (2011), which limits the amount that employers have to pay to a maximum of $2,217.60 per employee, regardless of salary. Individuals are also prevented from funding their CPP beyond this amount. But when it comes to the cost that you as the employer of the public sector have to pay, there is no limit!

Underfunded Pensions

As we have mentioned, taxpayers guarantee pension payments to public service workers. This means that if the fund investments don't meet expectations, or if pensioners live longer and thus payouts are higher than estimated (both of which occur in almost every public sector pension plan), the government has to top up the fund—with your tax dollars. This is done yearly, based on actuarial calculations. This shortfall amount is referred to as a pension deficit, or unfunded pension liability, and refers to the future benefit liabilities of the pension plan.

No one was particularly concerned about these deficits before the latest market collapse in 2008. But now that even our "too big to fail" industries are, in fact, failing, and in some cases going bankrupt, people are very concerned. Employer and employee contributions to pensions are invested with the expectation of capital growth to fund retirements. If stock markets move ever upward as they did in the 1980s and 1990s,[16] when baby boomers drove markets higher by investing hundreds of billions of their pension dollars into equities, no problem. If the boomers withdraw those hundreds of billions to support their retirements and the markets flatline as they did in the last decade, well, that's a problem. In fact, the markets may just follow Japan's lead, where an aging population, longer lifespans, and massive public debt have nudged Japanese stock markets downward for two decades with no rebound in sight. Big problem. And if people live longer, and if future economic growth is flat, and if the cost of living rises more than expected . . . meltdown.

Do defined benefit pensions and their associated liabilities represent a serious amount of money? Well it depends somewhat on the industry. Consider General Motors, for instance. When the company declared bankruptcy two years ago, GM Canada's pension deficit was $6 billion, meaning that sometime in the near future, as its workers retired, GM would need to come up with $6 billion from either profits or loans to pay defined benefits to workers who were no longer producing anything of value to the company. Ostensibly Canada's $10.6 billion bailout of GM was to save jobs, but in reality it may have been to save pensions. The bailout amounted to $2 million per job—hardly defensible under any business case scenario. The restructured GM will employ only 5,500 workers in Canada, down from 20,000 four years ago. Those 5,500 workers would have eventually found work elsewhere, but no one would have picked up the tab for the pensioners. Meanwhile other large companies, such as Air Canada, U.S. Steel, and Nortel were going bankrupt with no way to cover their pension deficits. U.S. Steel took a government handout based on job retention then promptly closed down anyway, leaving the government to pursue the steel giant in court for retribution. Typically these large bankrupt companies are broken up, with the pieces purchased by new owners who feel no obligation to workers from previous regimes. Paying pensions to former employees becomes a negotiable matter. And those negotiations rarely, if ever, favour the employee.

Problems in the private sector plans made media headlines, but pale in comparison to the unfunded liability in public sector plans. The amount of these liabilities is estimated at $300 billion and grows every year. Should you be concerned? If you are a taxpayer, yes sir, because you are on the hook for this $300 billion. If you work for the public sector, yes again, because your pension depends on either a government bailout every year, or higher pension contributions from union members who are still working.

Private sector taxpayers are just beginning to hear about these obligations and politicians are beginning to line up on one side or the other. Will they align themselves with the 20 per cent of Canadians who are eligible for these generous pensions or the 80 per cent of Canadians who are not? Which side has more supporters? When you consider that most politicians at every level make less money and have smaller pensions than the top civil servants they supposedly manage, it's not difficult to believe that people seeking office will side with the majority and seek a way to avoid this liability on behalf of the taxpayers. On the other hand, our current politicians share the same pension plan as their civil servants, a major reason why they don't want to focus any attention on this issue. The main pension focus of our politicians is private sector pensions. They like their pensions, and just wish you could find a way to get one of your own without affecting theirs.

How to Miss the Point Completely

Despite being one of the biggest problems for governments across Canada, the question of public sector pension sustainability was not even discussed in the 2011 federal budget. The Québec government published an extensive report in March of 2011 on the QPP and reported that it is an unsustainable time bomb unless dramatic changes are made.[17] This excellent report pointed out the problems that an aging workforce brings. Québec's report outlined concerns about declining labour force participation rates, more retirees than workers, and contribution rates into the plan that are too low. The Québec government introduced a new Voluntary Retirement Savings Plan.[18]

Québec is not alone in its concern with pension problems. Four provinces recently held expert commissions, the federal government did two studies, and all of the provinces created special reports for the finance ministers' conference on pensions in 2010. Despite this intense focus, not a word was said about the 800-pound gorilla in the room: public sector pensions. Hundreds of thousands of dollars and thousands of hours were spent putting these reports together and the biggest retirement threat to taxpayers—public sector pensions—was not even mentioned?

Why are Public Sector Pensions Set at Seventy Per cent?

Recent studies have concluded that the true amount necessary to maintain one's lifestyle after retirement is not 70 per cent of salary, but closer to

40–45 per cent for most people.[19] Seventy per cent was probably the highest number public sector unions could negotiate for their members while keeping a straight face and so the mythical figure was born.

You need much less income in retirement because many employee expenses are eliminated, including payroll deductions, such as CPP premiums at 4.95 per cent of income, Employment Insurance premiums at 1.73 per cent, and CPP and other workplace pension contributions, which can be as much as 10 per cent of the average income. These payroll deductions then can save retirees as much as 17 per cent.

There are many lifestyle expenses that are reduced in retirement, as well. The immediate ones that come to mind are transportation and parking for work, clothing, and meals. The single biggest such expense would be housing, as most Canadians over the age of 65 no longer have a mortgage. A StatsCan report in 2011 showed that 15.1 per cent of Canadians over the age of 65 still had a mortgage, compared to 86.9 per cent of those under 45.[20] Even for those over 65 with a mortgage, the mortgage costs were almost half of the Canadian average. Considering that $14,400 is the average annual mortgage payment for Canadians, the elimination of mortgages is a big factor in the disposable income of retired Canadians.[21]

As a result of reduced expenses, most public employees will retire with a higher disposable income than they had when they were working. It is interesting that the federal government, in its *Summary Report on Retirement Income Adequacy Research*,[22] noted that homes were a major source of income for retired Canadians. This means that some retirees might possibly have to sell their homes in order to afford retirement. For public sector workers this is not an issue, as comfortable pensions provide them with a higher disposable income than they likely had when they were working. In a pinch, they might have to sell the cottage.

Details from a report by Canadian pension expert Fred Vettese,[23] chief actuary with Morneau Shepell, covered this issue. The report uses the term "neutral retirement income target" (NRIT) to define the level of retirement income (from CPP, OAS, RRSPs, and pension plans) required to maintain the same disposable income after retirement. In Figure 2.1, the NRIT is indicated by the dotted line at 43 per cent of final pay.

FIGURE 2.1 Why Income Needs Drop in Retirement

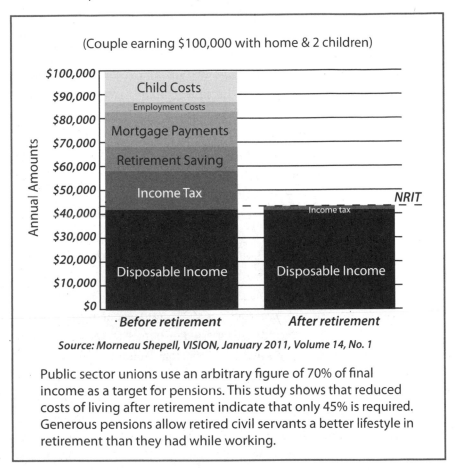

(Couple earning $100,000 with home & 2 children)

Source: Morneau Shepell, VISION, January 2011, Volume 14, No. 1

Public sector unions use an arbitrary figure of 70% of final income as a target for pensions. This study shows that reduced costs of living after retirement indicate that only 45% is required. Generous pensions allow retired civil servants a better lifestyle in retirement than they had while working.

Seniors also benefit from an income tax system that includes an age credit (starting at 65), a pension income credit, and the ability to split pension income or transfer credits between spouses. To achieve a target of 43 per cent of working income, a couple would each have had to save 6.5 cent of their pay for 35 years. This would entail a contribution of 3.25 per cent from both the employee and the employer, and would be much more sustainable for the economy.

Vettese points out that retirement planning is a balancing act, with the NRIT as the equilibrium point. Save too little and you won't have enough retirement income. Save too much and you will be depriving yourself unnecessarily during your working years. On the other hand, if we apply this analysis to the public sector, the 70 per cent rule used for pensions is unrealistic, unfair, and unsustainable for taxpayers.

Vettese's report shows, surprisingly, that the higher the level of income in working years, the lower the replacement income required in retirement. This highlights even more dramatically why the excessive pensions of top public sector income earners (in excess of $100,000) are so obscene. The income replacement number for homeowners with two children varies from 48 per cent of income at the high end to 40 per cent at the low end— both a long way from 70 per cent.

Public sector employees who qualify for the full 70 per cent of income-pension not only retire into the highest income levels in society, they also are able to travel, own second homes, and live a life of luxury. For most Canadians, this is a fantasy that will never come to pass.

One strategy you could consider is to move outside of Canada to a jurisdiction where you can live your fantasy life, pay much lower taxes, and live like a king. The Ontario Teachers' Pension Plan website informs retired teachers that they can have their pensions automatically deposited in a bank in Europe, Belize, or Costa Rica.[24]

What is a Fair Pension?

Before we go any further let's ask the question of what is fair in terms of pension amounts. As you saw in the story of Carl, Marnie, Mark, and Jennifer, people have worked side by side building this country only to arrive at dramatically different points as far as pensions go. Let's take a look at the couples' taxpayer guaranteed–pensions.

For simplicity's sake we have used CPP figures for 2010 for this illustration, as if the couples were all beginning to receive their pensions in that year. Carl, Mark, and Jennifer each qualified for the maximum CPP pension, since their incomes exceeded the maximum pensionable earning threshold of $48,300. Marnie's CPP would be approximately 65 per cent of this, based on an average income of $32,000. We have used an average final five years' salary of $130,000 for Mark as a senior civil servant and

	CPP	OAS	GIS	Pension	Total
Carl	$11,520	$6,312	$516	—	$ 18,348
Marnie	$ 7,488	$6,312	$516	—	$ 14,316
				Total	$ 32,664
Mark	$11,520	—	—	$79,480	$ 91,000
Jennifer	$11,520	—	—	$26,980	$ 38,500
				Total	$129,500

$55,000 for Jennifer. As you can see, Carl and Marnie qualify for additional OAS and GIS payments, but Mark and Jennifer do not.

The difference in the couples' annual benefits during the first year of retirement is $96,836. Since all of these pensions are indexed for inflation the gap will widen each year. If we use an inflation rate of 2 per cent, within two years this gap will reach more than $100,000. If we imagine that all four of our friends will live for 21 years after retirement, Mark and Jennifer will be receiving $196,279 per year in their final year, while Carl and Marnie will get $49,508—a difference of $146,771 per year!

And so we ask the question again, is there anything Mark and Jennifer can be doing in retirement that justifies them being paid $196,279 per year? At age 77? We think you can clearly see that these pensions are really deferred income, hidden from public view and taxed years after they were earned.

To make the life of pensioners easier, Canadian Finance Minister Jim Flaherty gave them a special break whereby they could split their income for tax purposes. When income splitting was introduced, the financial planning company Investors Group said that it was "one of the most significant changes to Canada's tax code in recent memory." Do you think this move was for the advantage of the 80 per cent of Canadians without pensions or to garner favour with the public sector unions?[25]

If Mark and Jennifer were to collect their full pensions for 30 years, the total income stream from their pensions will amount to $5.2 million if adjusted for inflation at 2 per cent. After 20 years, or at age 78, their annual income will be the same as it was just before they retired.

As we were writing this book, we contacted several public sector employees—some retired, some still working—to get a better understanding of their point of view. Naturally all of them consider their pensions to be just reward for their work. Many pointed out that they contributed to their pension funds and therefore owed nothing to taxpayers. They were often quick to blame politicians for poor decisions on taxpayers' behalf and often blamed the private sector for not paying higher pensions to its workers. They blamed governments—the very same ones that were protecting them—for not taxing industry higher, for using tax money to prop up failing businesses, and—this one's priceless—for paying senior public sector workers (but not themselves, of course) too much. This is to be expected; we could hardly expect people to say they were overpaid, that they didn't work hard enough, or that they are receiving too much money in retirement.

In isolation, of course, there is nothing to be gained by criticizing others for being successful. That being said, there is no isolation between public sector workers and the taxpayers who pay them. If our governments had operated with balanced budgets for the past 40 years we could rightly say that all is well and fair. However, an examination of the financial state of our governments shows that they have consistently borrowed money to pay out more than they—in other words, we—could afford, and have also committed future generations to fund pension liabilities, a debt they will be paying for years to come.

It is important to understand that we are not making value judgments about public employees. Is a teacher worth $50,000 a year, $60,000 a year, $120,000 a year? What about a garbage collector, a sewage worker, a building inspector, an arena manager? Our answer to that would be that public sector jobs are worth whatever we can afford to pay, but that we cannot afford to borrow money every year to underwrite these jobs and fund pensions for these workers. And that is what has been happening for most of the past 40 years.

3

THE ROLE OF THE UNIONS

Meticulous attention should be paid to the special relations and obligations of public servants to the public itself and to the Government . . . The process of collective bargaining, as usually understood, cannot be transplanted into the public service . . . a strike of public employees manifests nothing less than an intent on their part to obstruct the operations of government until their demands are satisfied. Such action looking toward the paralysis of government by those who have sworn to support it is unthinkable and intolerable.

President Franklin Delano Roosevelt, 1937

Consider the following statements:

"I love my job as a teacher; I can't imagine doing anything else."
"I love my job as a police officer; I can't imagine doing anything else."
"I love my job as a firefighter; I can't imagine doing anything else."
"I love my job as a coal miner; I can't imagine doing anything else."

Which of the above quotes is likely not true? Keep your answer in mind as we look at one of the key players in our discussion, the public sector employee unions.

If you do a quick search of the thousands of documents, articles, and blogs that have been written on the topic of public-sector compensation in the last few years, you will find over and over again that unions have been accused of creating unsustainable wage, benefit, and pension contracts. Let's take a look at the role that unions have played in this.

Are Unions Good for Canada?

From the United Food and Commercial Workers website:

Why Unions are Good for the Canadian Economy

Many historians credit unions with the rise of Canada's middle class and the general prosperity of the country. By helping more workers make decent wages with more job security, unions were largely responsible for stabilizing the economy and stimulating its growth. Because of unions, more working people could afford houses, better food, clothing, cars, and other consumer goods. Increasing demand for these things created more jobs and even more economic growth.

Better-paid and more secure workers could also pay more in taxes to support the growth of public services like schools, roads, clean water, police services, electricity, and health care. Even those who have never belonged to a union have benefited from their existence all their lives.[1]

So, those are good things, right? Shared prosperity for one and all and the growth of public services. By 1970, close to 30 per cent of the private sector workforce was enrolled in unions. This reflected the nature of our economy, based as it was on resources and manufacturing, with many jobs requiring hard physical labour and offering increased risk of shortened careers through injury or death. Forty years later the majority of private sector jobs are in service industries, union membership in Canada is down to 16 per cent of the private sector, and private sector unions are no longer a significant force in our economy. This trend is global in nature. In the

FIGURE 3.1 Where Trouble Lies[2]

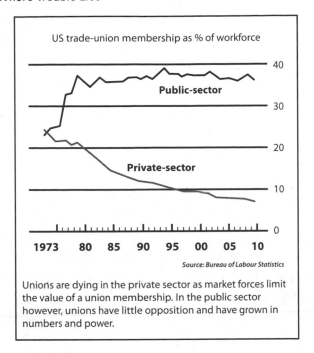

US trade-union membership as % of workforce

Public-sector

Private-sector

40

30

20

10

0

1973 80 85 90 95 00 05 10

Source: Bureau of Labour Statistics

Unions are dying in the private sector as market forces limit the value of a union membership. In the public sector however, unions have little opposition and have grown in numbers and power.

American private sector, trade-union density has fallen from a third in 1979 to just 7 per cent today. In Britain, once a hotbed of organized labour, the number has dropped from 44 to 15 per cent. Less than one-fifth of workers in OECD (Organization of Economic Co-Operation and Development) nations belong to unions.[3]

In the last half of the 20th century, unions had succeeded in raising the incomes and standard of living of their workers to the point where parents often told their children to "get a job with a large company, work there for a lifetime, and retire with a company pension." Although the nature of their work continued to be hard physical labour, unionized employees in the private sector made more money than their counterparts in the public sector and in non-unionized businesses.

In the area of pensions virtually all unionized workers were guaranteed defined benefit pensions as one of the rewards for a lifetime of building a profitable company. Today, however, with profits continually at risk from rapidly-changing market forces, virtually all private companies have moved to defined contribution pension plans for new employees, and most unions have accepted this as a necessary but unpopular concession to keep the company afloat and their members employed.

Public Sector Unions

How have public sector unions fared in these tumultuous times? What concessions have they made to ensure the long-term stability of their members' jobs and the survival of their employers? The correct answer would be, "Few, if any."

Of course public sector unions (PSUs) haven't had the same history as private sector unions. No child labour issues, no brutal work conditions, no thuggery on picket lines, no profit-hungry owners. PSUs developed in a comparative atmosphere of mutual support and respect. Even the decision to unionize was requested of, and supported by, the governments that employed them. Consider this summary of the founding of the Ontario Public Service Employees Union (OPSEU), originally called the Civil Service Association of Ontario (CSAO), from the OPSEU website.[4]

1911

The Civil Service Association of Ontario is created as a coal-buying co-operative and social club and to discuss ways of improving the civil service. About 200 people attend the initial meeting. Women are not invited. They agree to get the government's approval before proceeding further. The provincial government then had about 1,000 employees. Salaries were set by the lieutenant-governor. Pay increased with service, and long-term employees got first crack at promotions. There was no overtime. Ministers could fine staff up to $20 for misbehaviour. There was no appeal. There was no retirement age. A pension of one month's salary a year was granted to old-timers let go for ill health, and widows of career officials.

A lot has changed in 100 years. Twenty per cent of Ontario's civil servants attended the first CSAO meeting, but today approximately 70 per cent of all government workers are unionized,[5] with the remainder being seasonal or contract employees. In 1911, Ontario had 1,000 public sector workers. One hundred years later that number is 1,325,764, with a salary cost of $73.8 billion per year.[6] Across Canada the total government workforce is 3,604,999 people, or roughly 20 per cent[7] of all employees in the country. In Ontario for example, over 55 per cent of provincial government spending is on employee wages. When governments look for areas in which to control spending, they currently focus on infrastructure, taxes, grants, programs, and funding, but there is really only one place that meaningful cutbacks can occur, and that is the size and cost of the government workforce and its salaries, benefits, and pensions. Of the total 3.6 million government workers in Canada 3 million belong to a taxpayer-supported pension plan and 2.8 million of these are in a defined benefit plan.[8]

From a small group of people seeking a better price for coal and ways to "improve the civil service," we now have a massive group of highly-educated and highly-motivated people who seek to influence public policy to guarantee their job security, incomes, and pensions.

It's interesting to note the divergent paths taken by the private and public sector unions. Private sector unions fought for their creation and went on strike in the early years. Today they strike infrequently and most unions are happy to have their members working at all..Public sector unions spent most of their early years as part of the system working to "improve the civil service," but have more recently turned militant. Strikes, however, are on the decline. In 2005 there were 328 strikes in total in Canada; by 2010 the number had dropped to 175.[9]

In particular, PSUs have become highly politicized, spending millions of dollars to influence voters and elect politicians sympathetic to their causes. Note also that they have no party allegiance, freely supporting whichever party they believe will reward them most handsomely. CUPE, the Canadian Union for Public Employees, is particularly known for its political and social activism as noted by Wikipedia:[10]

[CUPE] has involved itself in broader struggles for social justice and equality, and emphasized the role of social unionism, as opposed to the more conservative business unionism practised by many North American unions. President Jeff Rose was known for outspoken opposition to Brian Mulroney-era wage restraint, free trade, the GST, privatization, deregulation, and cuts to public services. In 1991, Judy Darcy followed Rose and became the defining face of CUPE. One of Canada's most visible and colourful labour leaders, Darcy was a vigorous opponent of privatization, two-tier health care, and free trade agreements. Darcy was firmly committed to the union's involvement in broader social issues, and under her tenure CUPE strongly attacked the invasion of Iraq, condemned Canada's involvement in ballistic missile defense, and spoke out loudly in favour of same-sex marriage. Darcy stepped down in 2003 and was replaced by Paul Moist.

In May 2006, the Ontario wing of CUPE voted unanimously to pass a resolution to support the "international campaign of boycott, divestment, and sanctions against Israel until that state recognizes the Palestinian right to self-determination." This position was not supported by the CUPE national office.

As we can see, public sector unions have developed an agenda of their own that goes far beyond the traditional concerns of workers' rights, working conditions, and benefits. They have become a political entity in their own right, pushing an agenda that extends to foreign policy, marriage laws, free trade, sexism, child care, energy climate change, gender issues, highways and toll roads,[11] and anything else that strikes their fancy. Unions have become, like our political parties, largely independent of the people who elect their leaders. They clearly affect the results of our democratic process. Consider the millions they now spend on political campaigns. This is really your money, since it comes, ultimately, from the taxpayer. The unions' goals are to protect job security and secure higher salaries and lucrative benefits and pension packages for their members. These would also be paid for with your money.

Think we're exaggerating? In April 2011, the Ontario English Catholic Teacher's Association (OECTA) levied a $60 charge on its 45,000 members to create a $3-million advertising fund for an upcoming provincial election.[12] The move was opposed by 33 per cent of voting delegates, but the contribution was mandatory. So much for preserving the democracy of our political process. Teachers who may choose to vote Conservative or New Democrat in the election are now financing the Liberal's re-election campaign. Can you imagine a private corporation forcing its members to pay into a slush fund to support a specific political party? The campaign is being organized by a group called "Working Families." Working Families may sound like a group of parents getting together to fight for what's best for their children, but in reality it is an umbrella group of unions getting together to try and protect their incomes and pensions. Working Families[13] includes the OECTA, as well as the Ontario Secondary School Teachers' Federation, Elementary Teachers Federation of Ontario, Canadian Auto Workers, Ontario Nurses Association, Service Employees International Union, International Brotherhood of Boilermakers Local 128, The Millwrights, The Painters District Council Local 46, Ontario Pipe Trades Council, International Union of Operating Engineers Local 793, International Brotherhood of Electrical Workers, and the Provincial Building and Construction Trades Council.

The unions' goal is to ensure that Ontario Premier Dalton McGuinty's Liberals—known to be very favourable to teachers—get re-elected. To prevent undue influence of elections through vote-buying, strict laws are in place to limit the amount that political parties can spend on their campaigns. Currently however there are no limits on the amounts that external organizations can directly spend themselves to support or attack a political party before the "writ period." Third-party groups are prohibited from directly contributing more than $9,300 per year to the party and $6,200 to any particular riding association per year.

The $3 million raised in 2011 remains under the control of the OECTA and is therefore not subject to election spending laws. It can be spent in any way the OECTA chooses, to support the party provincially or to target key ridings. We're not convinced they have much to worry about. While McGuinty is considered pro-teacher because his wife is a teacher and his father was also, PC leader Tim Hudak has at least equal connections. According to a PC website, "Ontario PC Leader Tim Hudak understands the importance of classroom education because he comes from a family of school teachers. Tim's dad was a teacher and principal in the Catholic school system, his mother was a special-needs school teacher, and his sister has also been a teacher in the Catholic school system."[14]

As evidenced by OECTA's fund-raising, this union is very concerned about losing influence. Public sector unions will strike whenever necessary to achieve their goals. Unlike private sector strikes however, when PSUs strike it is not the owner who suffers (as FDR pointed out) it is the customer—which is you. When transit workers go on strike, the public is inconvenienced. When teachers strike, children are deprived of the opportunity to learn. When garbage workers strike, taxpayers must put up with rotting garbage in their homes and local parks. Whereas once our civil servants sought to "improve the civil service," now they seek to improve the rewards of being in the civil service.

Public sector unions have now become so powerful that they seek to influence a greater share of public sector spending, enforcement of wage settlements, benefits, pensions, and working conditions at all levels of government. Attempts to control the power of unions meet with strikes, work slowdowns, and huge advertising campaigns aimed at forcing elected officials to support union demands. Unions often allow contract negotiations to stall for months until a politically-opportune time (such as just before an election) creates the proper environment for a favourable outcome. Settlements are retroactive, so unionized employees never lose in this scenario.

To control this type of influence and pressuring of politicians, limits need to be placed on unions. Currently in Canada the activities of unions work within the bell jar into which no light can shine. There is no disclosure about the amount of money that unions raise, how it is spent, or how much they pay their leaders.

John Mortimer, a union watchdog with Labour Watch, a non-profit organization that educates workers who may not want to unionize, has shed some very alarming light on the situation in Canada. Labour Watch has attempted to uncover the extent of union influence in Canada and found it a very daunting task. The amount of union dues paid in Canada is unknown but estimated in the hundreds of millions of dollars. Imagine 3.6 million government workers earning $60,000 per year, all paying 1–2 per cent every year in union dues. It adds up to a lot of money.

In his attempts to uncover the activities of unions, Mortimer regularly refers to the United States Department of Labor disclosure statements by unions. The U.S. requires unions to file financial reports, disclose activities and expenses, and publicly list the salaries of senior union bosses. None of these requirements exist for Canadian unions, and the mandating of similar information is an important step that must be undertaken to protect taxpayers in Canada.

If all other measures fail, contract disputes go to arbitration, where highly-paid lawyers and former civil servants have absolute authority to impose a resolution on the taxpayer. In most cases, arbitrators award settlements higher than those that have been negotiated in the past without arbitration. Arbitrators are usually better paid than the employee groups whose wages they are arbitrating, so it is easy to see why they might side with the employees. If you are an arbitrator earning $150,000 a year, a request to grant a 3 per cent raise to workers making $65,000 might not seem unreasonable. Politicians are often quoted as defending the high increases awarded to the public sector by suggesting that the only alternative would be arbitration, and they feared the awards there would be higher. Arbitrators, arbitrary? *Webster's Dictionary* defines arbitrary as "guided by will only; high-handed, despotic, absolute." In truth, there is no one who can be considered impartial in this situation. We all bring our own paradigm to the table, which is why a mandatory balanced budget must be the foundation of good government. Arbitration should start with the premise of "live within your means," and any arbitration award should be within current budgets, not added to current budgets, as is now the case. Arbitrators point to a lack of legislation in this area. It's time our government faced up to its responsibilities to the taxpayer and took control of this situation. We will discuss this further in Chapter 10.

The basis for most decisions in arbitration is called parity. Arbitrators look to other contracts negotiated in the civil service to decide on an appropriate settlement. This is a disaster for hospitals, universities, and cities because although their employees are paid by the municipality, they belong to provincial unions. This broader market comparison creates compensation awards based on the wealthiest cities in the province. These contracts are then beyond the control of employers, and their needs (or budgets) are not taken into consideration. Settlements for workers need to be determined on the ability of each municipal employer to pay, and not on what other communities can afford.

Unions have an unfair advantage which costs taxpayers more than they should have to pay. They have full-time staff whose only job is to negotiate and lobby for better benefits, dealing with government negotiators who have no power to enforce settlements. In negotiations, unions present examples of the highest labour settlements they can find and if all else fails, they go to labour-friendly arbitrators to ratify contracts based on these "parity" demands.

This system is failing Canadians and it must be changed. Disclosure laws need to be implemented to expose the inner machinery of the unions and the arbitration system. Arbitration needs to be amended to take into account taxpayers' interests and not just those of the union.

We now have a government "of the employees, by the employees, for the employees."

We can see also that this has not always been the case. The OPSEU website notes that "The Great Depression leaves anyone with a job feeling pretty lucky. Ontario civil servants accept wage rollbacks to retain their jobs as the country goes through an economic upheaval." This is from the 1930s. Will we experience déjà vu in 2011? We doubt it.

Teachers and Their Pensions

Let's take a look at a typical public sector pension and see how it has evolved over the years. We'll use the Ontario Teachers' Pension Plan (OTPP) as our example. When it started in 1917, the OTPP offered teachers who had been working for 40 years a pension of $1,000 per year.[15] It was not until 1933 that that amount was increased to $1,250. In 1945 the pension was increased to a maximum of $1,500 for teachers who had 36 years of service and were 65 (men) or 62 (women) years of age. By 1954 teachers had eliminated the $3,000 annual cap on pensions and the pension was based on the last 10 years' average salary.

None of this could be considered particularly spectacular although signs of things to come were evident. In 1965 retirement with a pension was allowed at age 55, a full 10 years before most Canadians could retire. After that it was a matter of ratcheting up the annual pension income that would be received. The OTPP pension was no longer a simple means of staving off poverty in old age, but became a tool to find new ways of creating wealth for retiring teachers.

In 1971 survivors were added to the pension plan, so that if a teacher on pension passed away before his spouse, his spouse would continue to receive a pension, usually about 60 per cent of the previous total, until she died. In couples where both husband and wife were teachers, the survivor got to keep both pensions when the spouse died. In 1971 it was still common for one parent to be the main breadwinner and the other parent to be at home raising children, so the spousal survivor benefit made a lot of sense, preventing homemakers from becoming penniless widows upon the untimely death of their partner. Today, of course, it is rare to find a home in which both parents are not fully employed, but this spousal benefit has never been removed from any public sector pension.

New pension "windows" were opened up. These windows allowed teachers who had not yet qualified for their full pension to get one based on a combination of minimum years of working and age. For example, the first window in 1986 provided for an unreduced pension for pension plan members who were aged 55 with at least 10 years of service. In 1998 the "85 factor" was introduced as a "temporary" measure and was converted a few years later into a permanent benefit. It allowed anyone who had a combination of years worked plus age totalling 85 to retire on full pension. For example, a 55-year-old teacher with 30 years and a 65-year-old teacher with 20 years of classroom time would both be fully qualified for a pension. The most recent OTTP goodie was to base pensions on the highest or best five years of salary, rather than on average earnings. This again is a benefit that does not occur in the private sector and substantially raised pension income for retired teachers. (See Chapter 2 for an example of how much difference this single benefit makes.)

Based on the current salary grid in the province of Ontario, many teachers will be retiring with a salary in excess of $90,000 per year. The salary grid is the practice of automatically advancing up the pay scale by moving to a new job classification or getting an increased salary based on simply having worked another year in the same job, doing the same work. A school board may claim to be limiting union raises to 3 per cent; this figure applies to the annual base salaries in the contract but in reality, the total cost is higher because some employees have moved up to the next grid level of seniority or have been promoted to the next pay level. The total compensation may reach 5–6 per cent even though the announced "contract settlement" was for only 3 per cent. Politicians use the lower number to promote themselves as representing the taxpayer by "holding the line" on staff costs. Then the multiplier effect of the additional benefits and pensions based on the true salary increases kicks in as well. So when you read "3 per cent wage increase," think 5–6 per cent out of your pocket and into theirs. A 70 per cent pension will give them a pension income starting at around $63,000 per year, including CPP.

These levels of income are well above the average worker's wage in Canada of around $46,000[16] per year. Not the worker's pension, mind you, the worker's wage. These pensions put retired teachers into the top 20 per cent of senior incomes.

The amount of lump sum value of a pension of a mid-level public sector employee is in the range of $600,00 to $1.3 million.[17] This is the total liability of the taxpayer. If the pension fund is short—and the OTPP declared a $17.2 billion shortfall in 2011—the fund can ask the taxpayer to make up the difference. The plan paid out $1.8 billion more in 2010 than it collected from employees, and this gap is expected to grow to $5.3 billion per year by 2030.[18]

An employee retiring at age 55, with a $63,000 pension has a life expectancy of another 29.8 years.[19] Assuming that the pension is adjusted for inflation at 2 per cent, the retiree will receive over $2.5 million in pension income based on normal life expectancy, and at the end of 29 years will have an income of more than $110,000 per year. Currently there is a dramatic trend to teachers living over 100 years of age. These employees will earn over $4.6 million, with about $856,000 coming from the CPP program assuming indexing of 2 per cent.

In the meantime, the workload of teachers has been reduced. As we know, teachers have always received about three months' holiday a year, when summer vacation and Christmas and March breaks are added up, so their salary is really for three-quarters of a year. This effectively takes a $90,000 salary to the equivalent of $120,000 a year, based on the number of weeks worked. In addition to that, we have seen teaching days shortened by 30–60 minutes a day. We have also seen a move toward dramatically smaller class sizes. Despite declining enrollments across the country we have not seen corresponding reductions in the cost of our education system, because potential savings have been consumed by these adjustments to teaching conditions. Nor will we see reductions. There are currently some pension plans that have only 1.5 teachers working for every retired teacher.[20] The teachers' pensions are underfunded, meaning that each year some of the current government budget (which is made up of your tax dollars) must go into the pension fund to top it up. Salaries and pension top-ups constitute over 75 per cent of the education budget.[21] As of 2010, on average, retiring teachers will work for 26 years but be paid pensions for 30 years.[22] Retirees in 1970 averaged only 20 years in retirement because lifespan was shorter and retirement later in life. In June 2011 the OTPP announced an agreement with the provincial government to eliminate the current $17.2 billion shortfall by increasing employee pension contributions by 1.1 per cent over three years.[23] Of course the teacher's contributions are tax-deductible from their income, whereas your contribution is . . . wait for it . . . just plain tax. So even though in principle the teachers are matching the taxpayers' contribution, in real terms you are paying more than your share.

To "Air" is Human, to Buyback Divine

Here's another interesting little twist the public sector unions have come up with and sold to senior bureaucrats and politicians that you probably didn't know about. It's called pension buyback or, in the U.S., "air time." This feature allows government workers to essentially buy pension-qualifying employment years, so that they can receive pension benefits for years they didn't actually work.

Pension managers claim that once invested, the payments will generate income sufficient to pay the higher benefits, but as we know, investment returns are unpredictable whereas pension payout is guaranteed by taxpayers. It has been estimated that the cost to taxpayers could be as high as $6 for every one dollar invested by a worker through a buyback.

Here's how the Public Works and Government Services Canada website[24] promotes the benefits of pension buybacks:

Advantages of buying back prior service include:

- increased pensionable service, which increases your pension;
- increased pension benefit for your survivors;
- the completion of 35 years of pensionable service at an earlier date; and
- the possibility of retiring earlier.

All pension benefits payable under the plan relate directly to service and salaries. As the number of years of pensionable service to your credit increases and you reach higher levels of salary, the pension benefits that you and your eligible survivors can expect to receive increase accordingly.

Note the terms "prior service" and the "completion" of pensionable service in the website notice above. We would suggest that "service" in this situation is actually no service at all, and that "completion" is actually the avoidance of completion. Even the term "buyback" suggests that the worker is "buying back" something that was hers but was lost or taken away. We guess the "advantages" of pension buyback all accrue to the worker, and none to the taxpayer. Almost all public sector unions have now included this option as one of their contract provisions. *Quelle surprise!* This is a great example of the one-sided nature of public sector compensation packages. Here's an example:

Pension Buyback Illustration

OMERS website

Lisa bought her two years of service at age 42, when she was earning $40,000 and had 12 years of Healthcare of Ontario Pension Plan (HOOPP) service.[25] Those two years would cost $9,200 using current buyback rates.

Assuming her average annualized earnings at retirement are $53,000, and that she lives until age 80, she will receive $602,100 in pension over her lifetime, compared to $539,700 without the buyback. For $9,200, Lisa receives $62,400 in additional pension— more than six times what she paid for the buyback. This does not include the annual cost-of-living adjustments that would be applied, making her real benefit even higher.[26]

In Sickness and in Health

Yes, there's more! Public sector employment contracts usually include the following: life insurance, extended medical plan, dental care plan, short-term disability, and long-term disability. Some of this, of course, is 100 per cent fully paid for by the taxpayer and in some plans retired employees pay 50 per cent. Through an accounting concept called OPEB, or other post-employment benefits, these benefits are extended from the moment of retirement until the retiree reaches 65. At this point universal senior benefits are provided by the provincial government, mainly prescription drugs. Some plans continue health coverage until death or the death of a surviving spouse.

Let's look at a typical "liability for sick leave benefit plan." Here's an excerpt from the City of Hamilton's employee contract with its librarians:

Under the sick leave benefit plan of the City, unused sick leave can accumulate and employees may become entitled to a cash payment when they leave the City's employment. An actuarial valuation as at [sic] December 31, 2009 has estimated the accrued benefit obligation at $39,292,000. Changes in valuation assumptions have resulted in an increase in the liability to $39,292,000 from the expected liability of $32,436,000.[27]

We would guess that one in a thousand taxpayers knows that cities, universities, hospitals, school boards, and colleges have these debts to employees simply because the workers didn't take time off for being sick. This, of course, is the complete opposite of employees who take sick days because they're entitled to them when they're not actually sick. But that's a whole other story. If you extrapolate the Hamilton numbers across the country, you will see that we have a $2.73 billion liability in our municipal public sector alone for this kind of sick leave benefit.

The liability for the aforementioned health, dental, and life insurance bridge benefits for Hamilton city workers who retire before the age of 65 is even uglier. As of December 31, 2009 the city estimated this cost at $101 million, an increase from the expected liability of only $74 million. The national liability for these bridge benefits at all government levels will be in the billions.[28]

In its financial statement Hamilton blames "changes in valuation assumptions" for the 21 per cent increase in liability. This probably reflects the concern that returns on investment in the future will not be as substantial as they have been in the past. It is these changes in valuation that think tank experts cite in charging that governments are understating the true size your funding liabilities.

Some of the other more notable OPEB expenses include the City of Toronto at $2.4 billion,[29] Hydro One at 980 million[30] and Ontario Power Generation at close to $2.3 billion.[31] Almost all of the government organizations we examined have these hidden liabilities. Taxpayers need to understand these hidden costs and hold politicians accountable. It is outrageous that taxpayers fund such juicy benefits for public sector employees especially when none of these benefits are offered to the average working Canadian.

A sampling of these benefits includes sick leave not taken, accrued vacation pay at retirement, health benefits, and severance or termination payouts at retirement. This burden needs to be eliminated from the taxpayers' pocketbook and these perks eliminated from government contracts. At the very least, the cost of health care must be shared with retirees. A report by the C.D. Howe Institute[32] suggests that Ottawa and federal employees were underfunding their employee pension plans by about 50 per cent of annual requirements, guaranteeing future funding shortfalls. The eventual shortfall will be picked up by taxpayers. "The federal government's net pension obligation under the fair-value approach stands at almost $208 billion—some $65 billion larger than reported in the Public Accounts," said the report. C.D. Howe says that contributions last year should have been 34 per cent of annual wages but that only 18 per cent was being contributed currently.

And then of course there's the "liability for vacation benefits." These are vacation days earned by employees as of December 31 of a given year but not taken until a later date. The Hamilton liability alone as of December 31, 2009 has been estimated at $23 million, or $1.6 billion nationwide.

The nationwide cost for these three liabilities alone—sick leave, bridge health benefits and unused vacation pay, just fringe benefits, if we use Hamilton's numbers as a benchmark—would total $11 billion and that's just for municipal employees. These municipal shortfalls will have to be made up through increased property taxes. Maybe in retirement we will see droves of people leaving cities and moving to rural areas where property taxes are lower, since these areas have fewer public service employees to care for 'til death do us part.

Portability

Pensions in the private sector were designed to create loyalty and retain trained and qualified staff within the company. Public sector pensions, on the other hand, allow total portability, meaning that you can take your pension with you wherever you go—from hospitals to universities, from cities to provinces, and even to the federal level. This allows workers to go wherever they can get the best deal—even in the same field—without their pensions being lowered. This may seem innocuous, but actually encourages competing departments in the same field, public works for instance, to outbid each other—with your money—to attract skilled staff from each other.

For instance, if you are a brilliant manager working in Lethbridge, Alberta and doing a great job for taxpayers there, the City of Calgary might offer you a higher salary to come work for it. In a private sector job, you would have to weigh the cost of losing ground in your accumulated pension credits, and might decide to stay put. In the public sector you would receive an increase in your pension by moving, since that pension is based on your highest average salary. This encourages a constant brain drain from one staff to another, incurring additional training and hiring costs without any benefit to the taxpayer. Buybacks and portability are not provisions that are available to private sector workers—yet another reason why public sector compensation is out of step with the private sector.

Spiking Pensions

It was common practice in many plans for employees in their final years to spike or "boost" their incomes by working overtime, since this extra income was included in pension calculations. In some cases workers could boost their pensions to 100 per cent of their salary. In 2010 the City of Fredericton investigated a serious problem it had with its employee pension plan. The plan was only 80 per cent funded. One of the key problems was that overtime was allowed to be used in the final average salary calculation.[33]

When the City of Winnipeg conducted an overtime audit they discovered that most of the overtime was going to seniors employees who also earned the highest salaries. Seniors employees got first opportunity on any overtime that was offered as a result of union seniority rules. Rather than having a policy of giving overtime to the lowest wage employees they ended up using the highest wage employees. If pension spiking is included in the pension calculation the cost of the pension is driven up in addition to the premium wages that are paid. In an unrelated issue Winnipeg discovered possible collusion between workers whereby one worker would call in sick, allowing a co-worker to book the overtime. Of course the worker calling in sick would be taking a paid sick day.[34]

Where the worst abuses have been found in the public sector are in cases where a senior employee has complete discrepancy over the level of overtime worked. Without pension disclosure in Canada it is impossible to determine the full extent of this pension abuse, however in the U.S. where they do have pension disclosure laws, some employees have pensions that exceed their base salary. In some instances retiring allowances, sick-pay payouts and vacation time payouts have been used in the pension calculation.

Accrual Rate Changes

When the public sector wants to juice up its pensions it can change the accrual rate, as mentioned in Chapter 2. This is how public safety employees (police, firefighters, and military) have arranged to retire on full pension income at an even earlier age than other public sector workers. Recent changes to the British Columbia pension act,[35] for example, changed the accrual rate for safety workers to 2.33 per cent. Most provinces have changed pension laws to follow suit. This had the effect of giving these workers a full pension after only 30 years of working. Using the pension formula 30 years times 2.33 per cent, yields 69.9 per cent. At 30 years of service, public safety workers will be eligible for the 70 per cent of income pension, instead of having to work for 35 years using the standard 2 per cent accrual rate. This resulted in a huge retroactive increase in pensions and the huge costs associated with them, picked up course by taxpayers.[36]

Once this change was made for police and firefighters, unions then proceeded to obtain these same benefits for other workers. Paramedics and correctional officers in Ontario became eligible soon after, and then there was a campaign by the unions to bring on probation and parole officers, sheriffs, highway safety officers, and conservation officers. We are waiting for them to include dog catchers on this list. After all, dog catchers are exposed to a public safety risk, trying to catch dogs on the loose!

These accrual rate changes to engineer earlier retirement ages with full benefits fly in the face of worldwide government policies that are delaying retirement for private sector workers. Greece, for instance, recently raised its early retirement option to 63 from 58, while France increased its retirement age by two years to 62. Canada cannot avoid raising its retirement age but these changes will not apply to the public sector, whose employees currently become eligible for pensions at 55, or 50 in public safety jobs, or when their age and service adds up to 85 for teachers. Federal politicians are eligible for pensions at age 55.

Consider the following conclusions from the United Nations:

- By 2050, the number of older people in the world (aged 60 and over) will exceed the number of younger people (under age 15) for the first time in history.
- Globally, there are now 629 million people aged 60 and over. By 2050, there will be two billion.
- In 1950, for every senior citizen (aged 65 and above), there were 12 people aged 15–64. By 2050, the ratio will have plummeted to one to four.

- The "oldest old" (those aged 80 and above) are the fastest-growing age group in the world. Their numbers are rising by 3.8 per cent a year.
- The number of centenarians (aged 100 years or older) is projected to increase 15-fold, from 210,000 this year to 3.2 million people in 2050.[37]

The UN says the "historic crossover" from the young to the old is so profound that it parallels the magnitude of the Industrial Revolution. In Canada, the federal government just made accrual rate changes to the CPP which punish private sector workers who retire early, thereby reducing their CPP payments. Interestingly, these changes do not apply to government workers, and the protected class of employees. So *you* are expected to work longer to earn more taxable income that can be siphoned off to pay for *them* to retire earlier. The age for regular retirement in the public sector needs to be raised to 65 for full benefits, with penalties for early retirement. This, we are sure you agree, would be fair to all taxpayers.

Firefighters and the military have an unusual situation. Generally, they are paid for simply being on call, should they be needed. Canada hasn't been invaded for 200 years, but "standing on guard for thee" has become a fairly lucrative occupation for the 90,000 members of our armed forces. Canada's new foreign policy of sending troops to fight in Third World civil wars has put a small number of our forces at risk—the highest commitment of troops to Afghanistan at any one time was 3,800—and cost the lives of over 150 young men and women, but the majority of our forces have desk jobs and will never see fighting action. Those who do see combat receive additional danger pay as compensation—and not nearly enough, we might add—but to provide them full pensions five years earlier than other public sector workers and 15 years earlier than the general public is unjustified. The current military budget is $60 million per day,[38] an amazing amount for a government department that affects so few Canadians on a daily basis. Despite Canada's lack of enemies, defence spending has increased from 5.6 per cent of Federal Government expenditures in 1996–1997 to 7.7 per cent in 2010.

Firefighters are on call 24 hours a day, but if there's no firefighting to do, they often sleep regular hours at the station. They are actually paid to sleep, or rather, in the words of one official: "We are not paid to sleep, we are paid while sleeping, and that's a different thing."[39] Different words maybe, but same upshot. Recently, the fire departments of major cities have rearranged their schedules so that firefighters can "work" seven days straight, 24 hours a day, and have the rest of the month off.[40] Yet they are paid full-time wages, benefits, and pensions. Many run their own part-time businesses or do contract work on the side. After all, these are young, healthy men and women. What else would they do with three weeks off each month?

Fire departments claim they must recruit the "best and the brightest" and certainly there is danger in actually fighting a fire, but the public is not fooled by these claims. Vacancies in fire departments routinely attract thousands of applicants because the job is widely considered to be one of the best in the public sector, and that's saying something.

Sustainability of the Current System

The three biggest pension plans in Ontario are those of Ontario teachers (OTPP), municipal workers (OMERS), and the health care system (HOOPP). Pension contributions for these three plans in Ontario have risen 400 per cent over the past 10 years. In 2000, Ontario taxpayers contributed just under $1 billion into these pension funds. This money is in addition to the yearly taxpayer contributions made as the employer-portion of their basic contract. In 2009 these plans required almost $4 billion—a 400 per cent increase in 10 years. And that's just in Ontario. As with all public sector pension plans, as increasing numbers of boomers retire, taxpayer contributions will escalate substantially.

4

POLITICIANS AND BUREAUCRATS
AT THE TROUGH

There is no valid reason why Canadian taxpayers are on the hook for public sector pension plans when in fact half of the Canadians working in the private sector will not even benefit from any private pension plan upon retirement. The unfairness has gone on long enough.

Canadian Federation of Independent Business,
"The Pension Predicament"

With complete control over all aspects of taxation and government revenue, and the task of simply deciding how to spend it, our government has been able to run up a $1.2-trillion debt on our behalf while making no one particularly happy (except themselves and their senior bureaucrats). As we saw in the last chapter, unions have succeeded in creating a veritable Land of Oz for themselves, where nothing is as it seems but everyone—in the public sector, anyway—gets what they want. Of course they continue to complain about everything—it's never enough—but if there are no complaints there is no need for a union, so complaints are just a smokescreen designed to distract taxpayers from coming to their senses. Unions, however, are just doing their job—trying to get the best deal for their constituents. There is no concern on their part about the cost to you, the taxpayer. What about the people who are on the other side of the bargaining table?

Who was negotiating on your behalf? As much as public sector workers and their unions are the obvious whipping boys, it's the elected representatives and the senior bureaucrats who are mostly to blame for our current predicament. They could have simply said no, we can't afford that.

Let's look at a few examples of waste and pension abuse by our politicians and leading civil servants. We think you'll agree that, in fact, these people are in the bell jar along with the rest of the public sector, and not on the outside with those who are footing the bill. The first example would seem to be relatively small potatoes, after all it's "only" $104,000, but this is a story that should cause all of us who are supporting the current system with our taxes and our votes to sit up and take notice. There are lessons to be learned.

It seems that the City of Ottawa's fraud and waste hotline received a complaint in early 2010 about auditor general Alain Lalonde[1] —the person responsible for keeping the city accountable to taxpayers, and also the person responsible for handling such complaints. The complaint was about a special $104,000 pension bonus given to Lalonde by City politicians. Prior to accepting the job at the City in 2004, Lalonde worked for the federal government and naturally had a federal employee's pension fund. He transferred this pension to the City of Ottawa employees pension fund. At the same time, using the special privilege available to government employees known as "buy-back" (which we explained previously) he invested some of his own cash to boost the value of his pension. He also had to add some money to make up for the difference in the value between the two pensions, since the City plan would pay him more than the federal pension. So far, this is just a story of a government employee taking advantage of some overly-generous retirement savings options. However, not satisfied with simply making an investment guaranteed by taxpayers, Lalonde went one step further and requested a refund for those payments and the income taxes he paid on them, even though he was not entitled to a refund. Stunningly, this request was approved by city councillors in 2009.

When challenged on the ethics of such a move, Lalonde hid behind a technicality. "At the end of the day, it was a decision of council, and nothing in the process was broken, so the rules were followed," he said.

Of course elected councils can make any decision they want, right or wrong. You might, however, hold the auditor general to a higher standard. Especially when there is a clear conflict of interest. In truth, councillors later realized the error of their ways—but hey, a decision is a decision, so they weren't about to rescind it, even if they did admit it was wrong. Besides, it's not coming out of their pockets. A number of city councillors told CBC News that they made a mistake in approving the payout. Some said they didn't really understand what they were voting for.

Three things come to mind after reading this account. The first is to question the ethics of Mr. Lalonde and how this might reflect on his ability to perform his duties as the auditor for all of Ottawa's other various expenditures. If he is comfortable asking for an extra $104,000 that he didn't earn and that was not in his contract, how can he be expected to be a reliable watchdog in similar circumstances that he may be investigating?

The second question is precedent. Once a precedent or benchmark has been established, all other public sector employees—all 3.6 million of them—have the right to expect the same treatment. So this $104,000 is merely the wedge to open the door for what could be billions of dollars of additional costs for taxpayers.

And thirdly, the rather shocking after-the-fact admission of councillors that they voted in favour of something they didn't understand, something they would vote against now that they do understand it.

Part of the problem with pensions is that they are very complicated. If taxpayers knew what was going on they would be outraged and upset enough to do something. Pensions are what some would call a "wicked problem." They are a wicked problem because there are so many ever-changing variables that affect the health of the pension. Changing one of the many variables in the pension may have unexpected consequences.

In the early days of pensions it was easy. There were lots of workers to pay into the plan, few retirees were drawing incomes, and stock markets were flying. That has all changed. Most defined benefit pensions are upside down, meaning they don't have enough money to pay the benefits they are obligated to. The financial problems of these government DB pensions have escalated because there has been a lack of focus on public sector pensions. No one in Canada has been looking at the big picture and the future financial problems we face. A full examination of pensions is urgently needed.

The UK commissioned the Hutton Report to look into the sustainability and future of public sector pensions. The Little Hoover Commission study in California was an initiative by the Governor of California to investigate the serious underfunding that exists in California's public sector pensions. Many other states in the U.S. have examined pensions. One key point that emerged from the investigations was that information about pensions is incomplete and benchmarks are lacking relative to similar types of pensions.

In the spring of 2011, the Public Employee Pension Transparency Act was brought forward to the House of Representatives in the U.S. The bill attempts to create transparency by establishing uniform reporting on government pensions at all levels. It would examine pension system calculations, and would develop estimates of liabilities using guidelines. All of this information would then be available on a central database available to the public.

A plan like this is needed in Canada. It would help politicians and other decision makers to be better informed and more qualified to make decisions about pensions. It is imperative that the federal government initiate an investigation into the country's pension funds, modeled on the many other reports from other countries. We will see later on in the book how most pensions around the developed world work in the same fashion. They target the same replacement income levels, generally 70 per cent of working wages, use the same formulas with the common being the last-5-year average salary, and fund under the DB pension model.

To Fire or not to Fire, That is the Question

Here's another one that defies logic. How do you get severance pay for being fired when, in fact, you *didn't* get fired?

In 2010 the Ontario government joined the rest of the country and folded their Provincial Sales Tax (PST) along with the Goods and Services

Tax (GST) into a new Harmonized Sales Tax (HST). This meant that PST collection staff were no longer needed, so they were given jobs as HST collectors. That sounds simple enough, right? Not so fast. Because they were leaving the employment of the Province, they were eligible for severance pay—up to 6 months of severance pay. Most of us might think they weren't actually being fired, but were rather being transferred—especially since their seniority, pensions and accumulated job benefits were being transferred along with the name plates on their desks.

So the story here is that 1,250 provincial government employees will all become federal government employees doing exactly the same jobs—and we're guessing with the same pay—but with different paperwork. (No guarantee on the salaries though, because our federal employees generally get paid more than provincial ones. They also have better pension plans, because the federal government pays about 70 per cent of total pension contributions, whereas the provincial government pays only 50 per cent.) They will not lose a single day of work but, because officially their "employer" is now a different level of government, they will receive severance pay equal to six months' work, as if they had actually become unemployed.

No mention is made in this story of loss of seniority, closing of pension plans, or any thought of opening the job competition for the new positions to other Canadians. Despite clear laws that require all government jobs be widely posted and advertised to attract the best people, these 1,250 provincial employees were guaranteed new jobs without having to worry about competition. But at the same time, they received their contractually-mandated severance payment as if they had been fired, at a cost of $25 million to you. So they were fired but not fired, get it?

In contrast, public servants in British Columbia who signed a similar deal to move to federal positions will not be entitled to severance payouts, so mark this as British Columbia taxpayers 1, Ontario taxpayers 0.

And so of course the spin doctoring began. In an article by Kenyon Wallace in the *National Post*,[2] Ontario Premier Dalton McGuinty defended the payments, saying his government has a responsibility to respect the contracts it signs, although he did admit there was an alternative.

"I guess the alternative is we could introduce legislation in the House and say, 'Look you signed a deal and we signed a deal. It is no longer convenient for us to respect that deal.' So, where does that take you?" Mr. McGuinty told reporters. "You know there's an important part of our brand as a province and as a government. When we do business with each other and do business with the world, when we give you our word, our word is our word."

Interpretation: It's only $25 million, so we couldn't be bothered inconveniencing anyone. These are our employees and we want to treat them better than anyone else in the world would ever treat their employees. A feature of our "brand as a province" is that we are really loose with taxpayers' money, so you will want to do business with us. Huh?

We think the alternative would be to do what's best for the taxpayers who elected you to govern in their best interests, and what is clearly fair and logical to everyone outside of the Ontario government, and not pay ridiculous bonuses to people for no good reason. But that's just us. We can guess, of course, that all seniority, vacation pay, sick days, and pension eligibility was transferred without loss from one level of government to the other.

Naturally there were complaints, but as per usual nothing changed. The Canadian Taxpayers Federation (CTF), as is often the case, took aim at the leader of the provincial Liberals without mentioning that 265 other elected representatives went along for the ride without a peep. "It's insane. The premier should not pay out a single penny, period," said former federal CTF director Kevin Gaudet. "For once the premier should stand up for the taxpayer instead of organized labour. It shouldn't be about funneling cash to his union buddies. It should be about people who pay taxes. Taxpayers already lose once with the HST. Now they're losing twice."

Further proving that our representatives don't understand who's footing the bill—remember, that would be you—the Ontario Ministry of Revenue said taxpayers won't actually lose the $25 million because the money for the payouts comes from taxes put aside every year to provide severance due to job loss and attrition.[3] Of course, in this case there was no severance or job loss or attrition, points that were conveniently ignored by the Ministry.

"This severance for 1,250 Ministry of Revenue employees who have been identified as impacted by the wind-down of the retail sales tax and the move to the HST is within this allocation and as such has no incremental cost to government," said Leslie O'Leary, a spokeswoman for then-Revenue Minister John Wilkinson.

Apparently being "impacted," which in this case meant switching to a new office, is so severe that it is considered worthy of $45,000 in compensation. And "no incremental cost to government" indicates simply that the government knew this payout was coming so it's no big surprise (to them) and therefore not worth reviewing. It's in the (big honking deficit) budget, so what's the big deal?

Ms. O'Leary said the one-time severance payout of $25 million should be contrasted with the $100 million in yearly savings the government expects under the HST due to lower salary and overhead costs. This explanation ignores the fact that the two amounts have nothing to do with each other, and is merely intended to give the impression that the $25 million will come from the $100 million in savings. Any way you want to spin it, the fact remains that this was an unnecessary expenditure of $25 million for absolutely no value, and that you paid the bill. Or at least you will when it comes due. With interest. It was actually part of the $19-billion deficit Ontario rang up in 2010. Remember that this is only the deficit for that year; Ontario is actually $200 billion in debt. The concept of deficits and debt confuses many people, including the reporters who provide us with news on Canada's finances.

"I'm Entitled to my Entitlements"

When coming up with examples of our public service perks train wreck, it's hard not to think of David Dingwall. Dingwall was first elected as a Liberal MP in 1980 for Cape Breton-East Richmond in Nova Scotia. He was re-elected in three subsequent elections, and served as Opposition House Leader from 1991 to 1993. In 1993 Dingwall was appointed to Cabinet as Minister for the Atlantic Canada Opportunities Agency, Minister of Public Works, and Minister of Supply and Services. In 1996, he was moved to the position of Minister of Health. He lost the 1997 election and left public office to form his own lobbying firm, returning to the public sector in 2003 as President and Chief Executive Officer of the Royal Canadian Mint.

Life was good for only two years, however, as Dingwall "resigned" or was forced from office in 2005, in the midst of a controversy concerning his expenses at the Mint. He was also under fire for failing to register as a lobbyist for a Toronto pharmaceutical company,[4] a role he played before joining the Mint. The company reportedly agreed to pay Dingwall up to $350,000 for his help in securing grants under the Technology Partnerships Canada program, despite the fact that program rules forbid companies from hiring lobbyists.

Dingwall's story is unfortunately not unusual in the world of unsupervised expense accounts that are a way of life in the public sector. In the fall of 2005, documents released by the Conservatives[5] showed that Dingwall and his top aides amassed office expenses of more than $740,000 in 2004. These included $130,000 for foreign and domestic travel, $14,000 for meals, and $11,000 for hospitality. Among the charged expenses were $1,400 for his membership at the Rivermead Golf Club, $5,900 in automobile expenses, and $1,500 in membership fees paid to the Nova Scotia Barristers' Society.

To be fair to Mr. Dingwall, an independent audit by auditing firm PricewaterhouseCoopers[6] found that "the expenses fell within the guidelines," and a second independent review by law firm Osler, Hoskin and Harcourt completely exonerated Dingwall. So it was within guidelines to charge taxpayers for golf memberships, law society fees, and, did we mention, $1.29 for a pack of gum. Apparently the guidelines for Crown corporation CEOs making $277,000 a year allow for taxpayers to pay for pretty much everything that passes through their hands or impacts their lives, even gum. Now that's cradle-to-grave protection!

So if we summarize the situation at this point, we can say that it is not a case of a bad person being bad, but rather of a good person in a bad system; a system that is designed to encourage the maximum benefit for people inside the bell jar at the expense of those on the outside who are paying the freight. And that's the way it is throughout the public sector. Everyone is encouraged and supported to bilk the customer—you—of every single penny, perk, pension, and pack of gum. It's all "within the guidelines." We believe the guidelines should be changed. Now.

Dingwall further polished his public image by testifying that he resigned voluntarily after the controversy erupted over his illegal lobbying and questionable expense account claims. Former Prime Minister Paul Martin and former Revenue Minister John McCallum also insisted that this was the case. Then, just as we were starting to like the guy, Dingwall undermined everything he had said by suing the government for severance pay, claiming he had been fired. Dingwall apparently changed his mind about his original exit strategy when he realized he was going to miss out on the biggest perk of all—severance pay and a bigger pension. The arbitrator, retired superior court judge George Adams, found the government essentially forced Dingwall out and awarded him $417,780, along with associated pension benefits.[7]

When questioned while giving testimony before Parliament as to why he felt he should receive a severance package after the voluntary resignation, Dingwall remarked, "I'm entitled to my entitlements," a statement that has come to represent the actions of public servants across the land.

Opposition MPs, led by Prime Minister Stephen Harper, were quick to jump on Dingwall's backtracking.[8]

"After months of evasive answers in the House of Commons, we have now learned that David Dingwall's departure from the Royal Canadian Mint was involuntary," Harper said in a news release. "This is contrary to the information given by the Liberal government. I am very disappointed that Parliament was misled on this matter."

Conservative MP Jason Kenney went further, telling CTV: "They lied to Canadians about the fact that he was fired and didn't resign. It's very strange. They just didn't tell the truth."

What's Good for the Goose . . .

Thankfully for Mr. Harper his memory is short. Fast-forward to March 2011 and we find Harper's Conservatives embroiled in exactly the same controversy. In 2007 Harper had awarded lifetime federal employee Christiane Ouimet a seven-year contract as public sector integrity commissioner, giving her an $11-million budget and approximately $200,000 a year in salary (and a staff of 22)[9] to protect public servants who blow the whistle on wrongdoing within the federal government from being harassed or punished for bringing these cases to the public's attention. (This sounds like a great idea—we're excited!) After more than three years in the position, Ms. Ouimet had investigated only five of 228 complaints filed with her office. No charges were ever laid. (This sounds like our government in action. We're disappointed . . . again!) In one celebrated case, Canadian Forces veteran Sean Bruyea's complaint was dismissed by Ouimet's office, but eventually won a federal apology and an out-of-court settlement after it was determined that Veterans Affairs Canada officials had shared his sensitive personal and medical information.

Ouimet was under investigation by Auditor General Sheila Fraser when the integrity commissioner abruptly resigned. It was later discovered that Ouimet had been given a secret severance of $534,000 by the Privy Council (the government's top bureaucratic office),[10] with a signed agreement that bound her to secrecy on the matter. This means she was fired, or as they say in Ottawa, "forced out," (as in, forced out of the bell jar). At the same time, it was announced that Ouimet was retiring, when she resigned her post. Who can keep track anymore? According to a CBC report, 18 of the 22 members of her staff had left in the previous year, and complaints from some of them about Ouimet's abusive management style triggered the auditor general's investigation. Fraser's report alleged that Ouimet had berated, intimidated, yelled at, and sworn at her staff. Ouimet denied these charges.

Interestingly, considering that Ouimet's work could be best described as non-offensive, she said she received many threats during her tenure, including one in which the Ottawa police spoke with an anonymous caller who used obscene language and said Ouimet would get a bullet through the head.

Ouimet's severance payment was made in October 2010 but didn't become public knowledge until months later, after the Commons public accounts committee demanded the release of Privy Council documents relating to the case. Ms. Ouimet had refused several requests to appear before the committee to defend herself against the auditor's charges and explain her department's lack of meaningful activity.

Harper said the payment to get Ouimet to leave was "the best, cheapest, and fastest way to make a change." Of course, she also gets a pension, having worked for 28 years for the federal government. Since Ouimet's pension is based on her final five years of income, and her role as integrity commissioner was her highest-paid position, she will probably make much more in retirement than she ever did when she was working.

Harper claimed that the government had no legal authority to fire Ms. Ouimet, because as we know, neither incompetence nor lack of achievement is cause for anyone to lose their job in the public sector. According to media reports, however, the Public Servants Disclosure Protection Act[11] says that Ms. Ouimet could be removed for cause at any time with the approval of the Senate and House of Commons. Of course that would have exposed her office to further examination, and hey, why bother going through all that when you can just give someone half a million bucks of taxpayers' money and let her ride off into the sunset and collect her pension?

The fact that Harper's Privy Council office could make such a payment without automatic disclosure to Parliament makes one wonder how many other skeletons are in the closet. And when Ouimet finally did attend her hearing, she told the committee that she was in the process of retiring anyway because Fraser's investigation was too "invasive" and "demanding." So if Harper had waited just another month or two we could have saved $530,000. We're just saying.

Of course you could write volumes about political scandals and the billions and billions of dollars that have been spent or misappropriated on departments, projects, and programs that any right-thinking taxpayer would have never approved. Let's now turn our attention to the politicians themselves. How are they faring in this winner-take-all game of blind man's bluff?

The Gravy Train of Pensions
New Brunswick

We mentioned the pension payouts of the retiring and defeated politicians from the 2011 federal election earlier, but this is not the first time the gravy train of pensions has been re-engineered in their favour. Let's take a look at a few other excellent examples.

At the provincial level, the most recent group to rejig the system were New Brunswick's Members of the Legislative Assembly (MLAs). In 2008,

MLAs converted their tax-free expense accounts into salary, hiking their base salary to $85,000 from $45,757. While this money ostensibly became taxable, in actual fact the expense money would be largely tax deductible against the expenses it was originally designed to allow for—although money not spent would end up in MLAs' pockets instead of being returned, as is the case with expense accounts. The big bonus of this move, however, is that now those expense funds have become part of the base salary used to calculate their pensions. MLA pension accounts were flooded with millions of dollars because their pensions were now based on the higher "salary." Naturally there were calls for a review of this new plan, and the MLAs acknowledged that perhaps there should be, but then fought against the review for three years before public pressure forced their hand.

What did this mean in real numbers? Let's take the case of Liberal MLA Larry Kennedy (21 years in office), who would qualify for a $74,000-a-year pension if he retired (for a job that he originally agreed to do for $45,000), which is $30,000 more than he would have gotten before the increase. Conservative MLA Bev Harrison (20 years) would get $70,000 a year, Liberal Stuart Jamieson (19 years) $67,000, Conservative Dale Graham $60,000. The list goes on and on. Jamieson, Harrison, and Graham would have these amounts topped up by additional pension payments based on their terms as cabinet ministers. As you can see by the lengths of their terms in office, they have known for a long time what the structure of their pensions would be, so these increases amount to a massive tax grab on the way out the door for these veteran politicians.

Under the new rules they awarded themselves in an unrecorded vote, New Brunswick politicians qualify for a $30,600-a-year pension after only eight years of service, up from $16,500 under the old guidelines. MLAs who manage to stay in office for more than 15 years receive up to three-quarters of their salary, and those in office longer would receive even more. All pensions are fully indexed to inflation, up to 6 per cent, and payable from age 55 on—no need to wait until the age of 65 for these Canadians. The Canadian Taxpayers Federation reviewed the plan and found that for every pension dollar a politician contributes in New Brunswick, taxpayers chip in $7. If interest is factored in, the CTF says, taxpayers chip in closer to $16.[12]

In Nova Scotia the amount contributed by taxpayers jumps to $22 for each dollar MLAs pay into their pension plan.[13] MLA pensions in both provinces cost taxpayers approximately $8 million each year. Roughly 60 per cent of all Nova Scotia taxpayers do not have access to any kind of private pension.

The decision to convert expenses into salary in New Brunswick was based on an independent review by Justice Patrick Ryan. Ryan made several recommendations, including an immediate review of pensions. In an unrecorded vote politicians ignored this advice, approving every measure in the report except the one dealing with pensions. Despite immediate calls for a review, it took three years of public pressure before the legislature agreed to take a second look.

The new recommendations decrease by one-third the amount paid to MLAs and ministers, but also reduce the service period from eight to six years. Under the new plan a member who served for six years would get $20,400 annually upon retirement. That would be down from the $30,600, but still higher than the $16,325 the MLA would have received prior to 2008—a 25 per cent increase. To put this in perspective, if an MLA was elected at age 47, served for eight years, and retired, he would be paid approximately $450,000 while in office. If he lived to 78 he would receive 23 years of pension, which comes to $469,000. Combined with his previous salary, this is effectively $919,000 for eight years of work. So in reality (the world you and I live in) this MLA is earning $115,000 per year, but half of it is deferred and indexed for inflation to reduce taxes and hide it from scrutiny.

New Brunswick NDP Leader Dominic Cardy criticized the reduced recommendations as not going far enough. "We want the MLAs to get a fair pension, but not something that's exorbitant," Mr. Cardy said. "It's not reasonable to make it even easier to collect public money."

British Columbia

It seems that 2007 was a good year to be a provincial politician. Not only did the New Brunswick MLAs improve their finances tremendously, their brethren in British Columbia did the same. After a three-month review by a randomly-chosen panel of low-income B.C. taxpayers—kidding!—a three-month review by a hand-picked and well-paid ($75,000 each), government-appointed, three-member panel, B.C. legislators accepted an average increase of 29 per cent in their base salary.[14] The starting salary for an MLA in B.C. rose to $96,892. Premier Gordon Campbell received a 48 per cent increase, taking him to $187,000 annually. Senior Liberals Gordon Hogg and Kevin Krueger received 41 per cent increases.

British Columbia's Opposition New Democratic Party members gave lip service to the idea of refusing the raise and giving the money to charity, but eventually caved in to their own greed and accepted it. Carole James, former leader of the official Opposition and the NDP, had her pay hiked from $120,762 to $145,373—a raise of $24,611, or 20.4 per cent.[15] Naturally, as we have seen in New Brunswick, this also created a huge boost in the value of the MLAs' pensions.

In another clever sleight-of-hand, MLAs included a buyback or "air time" provision which allowed them to buy $5 worth of unearned or ret-roactive pension eligibility for $1, with taxpayers picking up the other $4. Once again the six years in office requirement was enacted, which meant that the 36 Liberals and five New Democrats who were eligible received a retroactive pension bonus worth an average of $829,000. If all eligible MLAs exercised their buyback option, it would cost taxpayers an additional $34 million for past governance.

Shortly thereafter MLAs increased the pay level of 158 senior bureaucrats by an average of $20,000, at a cost of $3.15 million annually. Forty-one deputy ministers had their pay lifted to an average of nearly $218,000 annually, while 117 assistant deputy ministers were boosted to a yearly average of $158,000.

Of course, these legislators are probably working harder than ever so they deserve much more money than they were paid in the past, right? Wrong. The number of days the B.C. Legislature sits has actually been on a downward curve for the past 25 years,[16] according to political consultant Will McMartin. McMartin notes that the number of legislative sitting days per year was 102 in 1973, 108 in 1974, increased to 136 days in 1977, then dropped to 119 days in 1980. By 2005 sitting days were down to 52, and in 2006 members were in the House for only 46 days. Of course it's true that politicians spend time in their own ridings, listening to the concerns of their local constituents, but it's hard not to believe that B.C. politicians are getting paid a lot more to do a lot less than they ever have in the past.

Don't Forget our Illustrious Senators

The dispute over the value of the Senate to Canadians has been going on for decades. So go ahead—debate amongst yourselves, because no one in Ottawa gives a damn what you think about it. The Senate is the highest level of Canadian government below the Queen. And like the Queen, senators are not elected. They are outside the democratic process, existing through a vestige of entitlement whereby the ruling party can reward whoever it likes with oodles of your money for life.

Officially, the Senate has the final say on all legislation, and could, if it ever wanted to, stop bills from being passed into law. Of course, if senators did that the ruling party would get rid of them, so they don't really bother with that role. They simply rubber-stamp what elected politicians have decided, make a few statements here and there, show up at the best parties, and take long holidays. For this, they are paid by you. Very well paid, in fact.

Take Senator Raymond Lavigne for instance. Mr. Lavigne, a former Liberal MP, was appointed to the Senate by Jean Chrétien in 2002. By 2005, however, his conduct came under scrutiny when he sent a staff member (yes, even though senators do little, they have staff on the public payroll—can't answer their own phones, you know) to chop down trees on his riverfront property in Wakefield, Québec. Unfortunately the staffer accidentally cut down trees on a neighbour's property. In the subsequent court case between the two neighbours it was discovered that the assistant was on the Senate clock (and thus payroll) while he was cutting the trees.[17] Former employees revealed that they had installed a door in Lavigne's house and were required to work out with him before dawn in hotel gyms, all while being paid by you.

Lavigne was expelled from the Liberal caucus in 2006, but continued to serve as a member of the Senate. The court case naturally dragged on for years, and was finally resolved in 2011 when Judge Robert Smith of the Ontario Superior Court found Lavigne guilty of fraud and breach of trust. He faces up to 14 years in prison but may not go for a while as the appeal process is expected to drag on for many more years at taxpayer expense.[18] The Senate, in its wisdom and deep regard for the taxpayer, immediately moved to suspend Lavigne's expense account. His expense account? That's right; since he was first charged in 2007, he has been barred from attending Senate proceedings, in fact, he hasn't been able to act as a senator for four years, but he continued to have access to his expense account, which he used to ring up more than $300,000 for office and travel expenses. And this is while being barred from doing any Senate business, remember.

And one day, maybe (but we're not holding our breath), Mr. Lavigne may actually lose his Senate salary. That's right—he has been paid to be a senator during the time that he has been barred from being a senator. The Senate cancelled his expense account after the judge's decision in 2011, but left him with his $132,000 yearly salary. If the courts sentence him to more than two years imprisonment, he will in fact lose his Senate seat and his income, but we wouldn't count on that. Expect a suspended sentence, but likely not in 2011. Lavigne is expected to appeal the decision. No report on how much the trial has cost us as taxpayers. The fraud amount is listed as $10,120. Apparently the rest of the $300,000 consisted of legitimate expenses for a suspended senator who had no legitimate Senate-related activities. (Update: Mr. Lavigne announced in May 2011 that he was retiring immediately from the Senate.) Apparently if sentenced to more than two years in prison while in office he would have lost his $69,000-a-year pension, so he's just going to take the money and run. Even if convicted for criminal acts the public sector pensions are protected and guaranteed to continue to be paid.

So, four years at $132,000 per, plus $300,000 in expenses, plus the court costs, plus $69,000 a year for the rest of his life . . . you do the math. Money well spent? Welcome to Canadian politics. There are 105 senators on the payroll as of 2011, at a cost of $13.9 million—not including those expense accounts. Here's a good indication of their activity: senators' seats are considered "vacant" and senators can be replaced if they miss every single meeting for two consecutive parliamentary sessions. So show up once a year and you get $132,000 (plus expenses) until mandatory retirement at age 75. Unless, of course, you are barred from attending (in which case the government will mail you the cheque at home).

5

ONTARIO HYDRO

Power to the People

In public sector America things just get better and better. The common presumption is that public servants forgo high wages in exchange for safe jobs and benefits. The reality is they get all three.
Stephane Fitch, *Forbes*, "Gilt-Edged Pensions"

If you are looking for a poster child for government interference, manipulation, error, and overpayment, you could find none better than the multiple-headed offspring of the former Ontario Hydro. Once lauded as a prime example of everything that is good about modern government, Ontario's convoluted electricity agencies now represent everything that has gone wrong in our country in the past 30 years. From massive cost overruns on capital projects and wildly-escalating consumer bills, to excessive salary and pension costs, huge payouts for disgraced former employees, to taxpayer subsidies for foreign companies and guaranteed power purchases at many times market value, this one has it all. Where to start?

History of Ontario Hydro
Niagara Falls has been used for power generation since the 1880s. Serbian inventor Nikola Tesla had used hydro power to illuminate the Falls in 1883,

then built the first significant hydroelectric system at Niagara Falls for the
Westinghouse Electric Company in 1895. It was operated by the privately-
owned Niagara Falls Power Company. Tesla invented alternating current,
known as AC, which is used around the world today. His American rival
Thomas Edison invented DC, or direct current, a competing technology that
lost out to Tesla in a protracted and bitter business battle. In one famous
confrontation, Edison publicly electrocuted an elephant using Tesla's
invention, to show the dangers of alternating current. But we digress.

In the first years of electricity generation, power was privately owned,
but in 1905 Ontario was given rights to the Canadian hydro flow at Niagara
Falls. In effect this gave the province control over electricity, a monopoly
which it still largely enjoys today, although the deregulation of the electrical system in 1998 has allowed private operators a role. In 1906 the Ontario
Power Commission was formed, renamed the Ontario Hydro Commission,
and eventually became known as Ontario Hydro.[1]

The move to take public control of the power generated by Niagara Falls
was spearheaded by Adam Beck, later knighted for his achievements. Beck
was a Conservative member of the Ontario Legislature at that time, while
also serving as the mayor of London, Ontario for three years. Despite being
a Conservative he was opposed to private ownership of the power industry.
He successfully established Ontario Hydro as a government department
with a mandate to provide power at cost. In 1906 he was appointed the first
chairman of the Commission. Beck, by the way, was a self-made business-
man who donated his public salary to charity.

By 1925 Ontario Hydro had created the world's largest hydroelectric
plant at Niagara Falls. In the 1950s Ontario Hydro built coal-fired generating stations, and in the 1960s began the development of nuclear power. Up
until that point Ontario had benefited from some of the cheapest and most
reliable power in the world. With the advent of nuclear power, however, all
of that began to change, as did the company's mandate. In 1972, the Power
Corporation Act converted Ontario Hydro into a Crown corporation. This
changed Ontario Hydro's role from providing "power at cost" to providing
power at a profit. Since profits would go to the Ontario government, this
seemed to be largely a bookkeeping change, but as we will see, this program went wildly off the tracks.

Nuclear energy was promoted as a non-polluting energy source for the future, except of course, for the minor inconvenience of having to dispose of spent uranium and the minor risk of exposure to contamination should anything go wrong with the plant (see: Chernobyl; Japan tsunami). As it turns out, nuclear plants are not profitable, and by 1998 Ontario Hydro was holding $38.1 billion of debt.[2] So much for providing power at a profit. Sir Adam Beck would have been spinning in his grave.

In 1998, the Conservative government of Premier Mike Harris passed the Energy Competition Act, allowing private companies to enter the hydro market. At the same time, the province split Ontario Hydro into five separate Crown corporations. These are Ontario Power Generation (OPG), which focuses on the generation of power; Hydro One, which handles transmission and distribution of power; the Independent Electricity System Operator (IESO), which controls the flow of electricity, balancing it according to supply and demand; the Electrical Safety Association (ESA), which focuses on safety; and the Ontario Electricity Financial Corporation (OEFC), which inherited $30.3 billion of Ontario Hydro's debt (leaving $7.8 billion as "stranded debt,"[3] which shows up on your monthly bill as a "debt reduction charge"), and is tasked with eliminating it.

If that isn't confusing enough, we now also have the Ontario Energy Board (OEB), which regulates the province's private electricity and natural gas providers and sets prices for everyone. We also have the Ontario Power Authority (OPA), which is positioned between the OEB and five partners listed above. A quick surf of OPA's website turns up no specific information about what it does, but yields this vision statement: "Leading Ontario in the development of North America's most reliable, cost-effective, and sustainable electricity system." If you have been following the news about Ontario's hydro prices in the last few years, you will know OPA is not doing a very good job in terms of fulfilling this vision.

Below this provincial government hierarchy are the 90 or so municipal utility companies that divert electricity to your home (Hydro One services most of rural Ontario directly). And then there are the private companies, the most significant of these being Bruce Power, a private corporation that produces approximately 20 per cent of Ontario's electricity. Bruce Power leases its main generation assets—the Bruce nuclear facilities—from OPG. Setting policy for all of these entities is the provincial Ministry of Energy.

Problems Times 5 or 7 or 90 . . .

If you've been following our story so far, you'll know that government agencies are not particularly efficient. So you will recognize that during the first 70 years of generating electricity, when there was only one Ontario Hydro, the company was a spectacular success story. Ontario was the envy of the world. With one of the cheapest energy sources in the world, Ontario was able to attract the lion's share of the country's heavy industry, offering high-paying and stable jobs in the automobile and steel industries and other areas of manufacturing. Southern Ontario became the engine of the nation's economy, and supported most of the other provinces through transfer payments.

Let's look at the cost of human resources involved in the new, no longer-streamlined structure of Ontario Hydro. As you know, every government-run enterprise requires a management team and a board of directors to supervise it, as well as a legion of office workers, accountants, various specialists, and other support staff. Whereas once it was only Ontario Hydro (OH), we now have OH (recently renamed Hydro One) plus OPG, the IESO, the ESA, the OEFC, the OEB, and the OPA. Naturally all of these need a CEO and a BOD (board of directors). So by splitting one organization into seven, the province increased the management cost of our hydro system sevenfold. You may have heard the expression that "a camel is a horse designed by a committee," Wikipedia explains this as a group of entities coming together to produce something in the presence of poor leadership. The defining characteristics of "design by committee" are needless complexity, internal inconsistency, logical flaws, banality, and the lack of a unifying vision. In this case, the committee took the horse—an entity that was well designed and operating efficiently—and turned it into a camel, ill suited for the task. (No offence to the camel.)

Just consider the bookkeeping and communication costs involved. These entities must all interact with each other, in many cases with one selling the other its service. So whereas one bookkeeping department used to look after all of the accounting, we now have Hydro One billing OPG, which is billing the OEFC, which is reporting back to the OPA, and so on. This kind of duplication at every level has driven up operating costs in ways that are totally unrelated to the cost of physically producing and distributing energy. Of course the story gets worse as we delve further into the details.

Once built, hydro-generating plants are designed to run without hands-on human input literally for generations, so you would think that there would be little requirement for highly-paid employees except, per-haps, in the supervision of the construction of these plants. How would you explain this, then? Each year the Ontario government publishes the so-called Sunshine List of every Ontario government worker paid more than $100,000 in salary. In 2009, more than 10,000 Hydro One and OPG workers made the list. That is more than $1 billion in salary costs for those employees alone. Insiders tell us that there are security guards making over $100,000. Hard to believe that this job couldn't be outsourced to a private company for less. These two companies had 17,517 employees at the end of 2009, so 57 per cent of the employees had a base salary higher than $100,000. Factor in the benefits package for health care, vacation pay, sick pay, the government's contribution to the pension plan, and the government guarantee of that plan—Hydro One's pension plan is underfunded to the tune of $300 million—and you have a perfect storm of unsustainable costs. Some 90 per cent of Hydro employees are covered by collective bargaining agreements. Even the OEB considers salary costs to be too high.[4] Before we go there though, let's look at the actual numbers of the Ontario Hydro pension plan. As you know, provincial pension funding claims to be a fifty-fifty split, with employees contributing 50 per cent from their lucrative compensation packages and taxpayers chipping in the other 50 per cent. Here are the actual numbers from recent years:

Ontario's Hydro One pension contributions

(all amounts in millions of dollars)[5]

	2006	2007	2008	2009	2010	Total
Employee	17	17	20	21	24	99
Taxpayer	86	95	101	112	191	585

Clearly this is not fifty-fifty. As you can see from the escalation in tax-payer contributions, this underfunding is heading for the moon as more and more of those $100,000-per-year employees retire with their $70,000-plus pensions and benefits, and are replaced with new employees who will also get pension funding.

Even insiders believe that OPG is overstaffed and overpaid and the utility has "largely failed to deliver" in keeping costs down. In a report on the nuclear division in March 2011,[6] the Ontario Energy Board said OPG had failed to deliver the savings requested by Ontario's Energy Minister and recommended a $145 million payroll deduction.

"The board is concerned with both the number of staff and the level of compensation paid in light of the overall performance of the nuclear business," the report said.

"For the nuclear business the evidence is clear that overall performance is poor in comparison to its peers and the staffing levels and compensation exceed the comparators. On this basis an adjustment is necessary to ensure the payment amounts are just and reasonable."

Don't expect that $145-million reduction any time soon, though. The staff is virtually all unionized and will never accept a pay cut without a lengthy fight. And the Liberal government has no interest in the issue because it is too busy investing in its latest vision, committing $7 billion of your money to the Korean company Samsung to harness the wind. No comments about hot air at Queen's Park, please. More likely the Liberals will fire a few OEB board members for bringing it to our attention.

Criticism and mismanagement is nothing new at OPG. In late 2003, the incoming Liberal government fired the three most senior executives at OPG on the heels of a report that the retrofit of a single reactor at the Pickering nuclear plant had come in $900 million over budget and three years behind schedule. The government also accepted the resignation of all remaining board members.[7]

In early 2011 most electrical providers in the provinces were found guilty by the OEB of overcharging their customers. The companies were fined some $18 million in costs and damages. They were then given permission by the OEB to overcharge these same customers again to recover the $18-million fine.[8] And the point of the fine was?

With today's muddled corporate structure, it's virtually impossible to know if Ontario's hydro system is operating at a profit or not. According to an article in the *Financial Post*, the combination of inside lending at artificially-low rates, stock market gains from investments, unfunded pension and benefits liabilities, and depreciating assets make it almost impossible to determine if OPG is profitable. The writer of the article, retired Canadian banker Parker Gallant, suggests that OPG actually lost $60 million on revenue of $5.6 billion.[9] He also notes that combined debt has reached $13 billion, up 10.4 per cent in one year, with OPG's debt at $4.1 billion as of December 31, 2009.[10] This debt compares to $53 million in March 2003, shortly after the company's previous debt load was moved to the Ontario Electricity Financial Corporation. So despite, or perhaps more realistically because of, the reorganization of Ontario Hydro, everything is going in the wrong direction.

Hydro One claimed record profits in 2010. As is usually the case when a government department turns a profit, it quickly invested the money in new capital spending and more employees, adding 300 new positions. Operating costs jumped 4 per cent and HO has unfunded pension liabilities of almost $300 million, resulting in a need to increase rates for both its transmission and distribution businesses.[11]

A final word from Mr. Gallant points out that OPG's "profit" in 2009 came from growth in the value of its nuclear waste management fund. Its what? Yes, each year money has to be set aside to pay for the eventual decommissioning of these nuclear plants and the disposal of spent fuel rods. This fund is invested and was valued at $10.2 billion on December 31, 2009, but this amount is offset by the projected decommissioning cost of $11.9 billion, or almost double the non-depreciated value ($6.7 billion) of the nuclear assets.[12] Interpretation: It costs more to get rid of a nuclear power plant than it does to build one, all the while running it at a deficit. Is this anyone's idea of good planning? These are the same people who are planning Ontario's entry into wind and solar power. Keep your fingers crossed.

So there you have a quick introduction to how a government can screw up even a monopoly and turn the ever-flowing waters of Niagara Falls into a deficit. But surely with all the bad news, and the massive $19-billion deficit of the provincial government, and the $200-billion provincial debt, those $100,000-plus employees would be willing to pitch in for the rest of us and accept McGuinty's proposed wage freeze for two years, don't you think? You are so naïve. Here is an excerpt from the February 2011 newsletter of the Society of Energy Professionals, the union that represents many of the OPG workers.

Arbitrator critiques govt policy, awards OPG raises

The Society of Energy Professionals/IFPTE Local 160, February 4, 2011

Against the will of the McGuinty government and its wage restraint policy, an arbitrator has awarded members of the Society's OPG Local a two-year collective agreement with salary increases totaling 6 per cent. The award also includes a break-through improvement to benefits—coverage for dental implants.

"Government wage-restraint pronouncements are of no binding force or effect and, given the specific factors under Article 15 that must govern my deliberation, they can be of no practical effect either," ruled arbitrator Kevin Burkett in a 26-page interest arbitration award. "There is no basis upon which to conclude that the members of this bargaining unit enjoy an absolute salary advantage that should act to moderate future salary increases."

"All the hard work we put into bargaining has really paid off," said Local VP Joseph Fierro. "This is a very good result for the employees we represent, and sets a terrific precedent for the Bruce Power and Nuclear Waste Management Organization Locals, who will be in arbitration later this year."

Last year, the Ontario Legislature approved the Public Sector Compensation Restraint to Protect Public Services Act, the flagship of its response to the economic downturn and the resulting ballooning government deficit. It froze the wages of non-union employees in both the public and wider public services, and set out that no money would be forthcoming for future wage increases for unionized employees. Strangely, though OPG and Hydro One revenues and rates have absolutely nothing to do with government spending deficits, both utilities were included in the ambit of the Act.

Arbitrator Burkett found the context in which the two parties were bargaining to be most unhelpful for the resolution of differences: "It should come as no surprise that the parties made very little progress in direct two-party negotiation. Once OPG made it known that it was seeking a zero net compensation agreement and that it would be maintaining that position throughout, there was no reason for the Society to moderate its position or to seriously consider the OPG demands designed to improve the efficiency of its operations. The effect of the government pronouncement and its direction to OPG was to 'freeze' the bargaining and thereby to prevent the parties from either moving to an agreement or at least prioritizing their respective bargaining positions."[13]

Take note of the disconnect between the union's position and the financial reality of the corporation for which its members work. The union says: "Strangely, though OPG and Hydro One revenues and rates have absolutely nothing to do with government spending deficits, both utilities were included in the ambit of the Act." The union members actually seem to have no understanding that their salaries, benefits, and pensions, which are guaranteed by the taxpayer, contribute to government-spending deficits. They have no understanding that a $300-million funding shortfall in their pension fund is part of the government deficit. This is not unusual. We constantly hear public sector union officials and public sector employees state, "We did not create the deficit, and therefore it should not be on our backs to repay it." This delusion is not limited to unionized public sector workers trying to defend their position. The vast majority of Canadians believe that government debt is the responsibility of the government and not their responsibility. In reality, of course, more than 50 per cent of all government expense is public sector compensation, so therefore it *is* the debt! And we will all be repaying it sooner or later.

Note also the arbitrator's position here. He can't see how employees making $100,000 plus benefits have an "absolute salary advantage," and he accepts the position that if the union is not going to get any more money it doesn't have to "seriously consider the OPG demands to improve efficiency." Shouldn't "improving efficiency" be part of everyone's job description? Did we mention that you're paying his salary, too?

The union newsletter also quoted Burkett as saying that OPG is "being forced to operate with one arm tied behind its back," because of government policies and practices in regard to the electricity industry. He noted that the Green Energy Act offers competing producers unfair advantages such as guaranteed contracts at significantly higher rates for their production than OPG gets. Apparently unaware that OPG is accumulating huge debts of its own, he noted that OPG "will remain a profitable enterprise capable of maintaining the relative compensation position of its employees."

The union newsletter mentions the Public Sector Compensation Restraint to Protect Public Services Act, passed in 2010. Let's take a look at that and see if it's the solution we are all seeking. This is from the Ontario government website:

Public Sector Compensation Restraint

Ontario has felt the effects of the global recession and is running a deficit in order to create jobs and protect our public services.

The McGuinty government is managing responsibly by controlling costs in one of its largest spending lines—compensation of public sector employees.

Everyone who is paid through taxpayer dollars is being asked to do their part. MPPs will lead by example with a three-year salary freeze.

The government has passed legislation that will freeze the compensation structures of non-bargaining political and Legislative Assembly staff for two years.

It will also freeze compensation plans for all non-bargaining employees in the broader public sector, including the Ontario Public Service, for two years. This will help redirect up to $750 million toward sustaining schools, hospitals and other public services.

For employees who bargain collectively, the government will respect all current collective agreements. When these agreements expire and new contracts are negotiated, the government will work with transfer payment partners and bargaining agents to seek agreements of at least two years' duration that do not include net compensation increases.

The fiscal plan provides no funding for compensation increases for future collective agreements.

It doesn't matter whether contracts expire next month, next year or the year after that—all employers and employee groups will be expected to do their part.

This is a balanced and responsible plan that requires employers and employee groups in the public sector to work together and do their part to sustain public services.[14]

We could have some fun questioning how a $19-billion deficit is "managing responsibly," but let's stay on topic. Non-unionized employees of the government were given an immediate wage freeze for two years. Unionized employees were asked to follow suit. As of this writing not a single union has picked up on the hint, and as we can see from the arbitration award for OPG workers, the province's arbitrators are not going along for the ride either. To be honest, $750 million out of a $19-billion deficit really wouldn't accomplish much anyway. What is clearly needed is a massive downsizing of government staff or a major cutback of programs, or both. Since 80 per cent of government employees are unionized, this wage freeze is mere window dressing.

Notice also the two caveats in the press release. It says that the Liberals' "balanced and responsible plan" requires employee groups to "work together" with employers, which they are clearly not doing. It also says that "the fiscal plan provides no funding for compensation increases," meaning such increases are not covered in the $19-billion deficit. So any contract negotiations that result in an increase will add to the budget deficit. Certainly Mr. McGuinty is accurate in the first sentence when he says Ontario is "running a deficit to protect our public services."

It's Better to be in Management

Is that the whole story? No, it is not. We haven't looked at management yet. All right, so you are paying the salaries of the people that are managing this mess, the ones who have managed to screw up a monopoly, run up continuous deficits of billions of dollars, and build dysfunctional nuclear power plants while committing you to overpay for energy from wind and solar plants for the rest of your life. What are they worth? How about the highest salaries for public sector employees in the entire country? That's right, now-retired OPG president Jim Hankinson was paid $2.15 million in 2009. Of course that was just salary, bonus, and other compensation. When we add in the pension benefit on that huge salary, the total is $3.45 million.[15] By comparison, Premier Dalton McGuinty took home only $208,974.

The 2009 annual executive compensation report for the OPG reveals how even when we think we are getting the whole story, we're not. The 2009 Sunshine List discloses the president and CEO's compensation as $2,150,115.69, with $2,632 in taxable benefits, but in reality, the tax hit is almost $3.5 million. Here is what Hankinson actually received in compensation:

Ontario Power Generation—Executive Compensation Report
President and CEO—(2008 earnings)[16]

Salary	$ 860,000
Bonus	$ 898,700
Pension value	$1,010,000
All other	$ 683,246
Total	$3,451,946

This exorbitant reward for incompetence won't happen again in the future, though. Former Energy Minister Dwight Duncan set up an expert panel to recommend a new method of determining the pay levels of public sector executives in the energy sector because the OPG compensation packages are too high. Whoops, our mistake. The panel was set up in 2006, so we guess Hankinson's "low" compensation was a recommendation of Duncan's experts. We wonder what his predecessors were paid.

Then again, there's no need to wonder. It's all public information, so we can just look it up; after all, it's your money they are being paid with. According to a Canadian Press article from June 26, 2007,[17] Hankinson's equal at Hydro One, CEO Tom Parkinson, was being paid an annual salary of $1.6 million plus expenses until he quit in in 2006 amid criticism of expense account "irregularities." To help ease the suffering and humiliation, Parkinson was given $3 million in severance pay. Prior to that, Parkinson's predecessor as Hydro One CEO, Eleanor Clitheroe, was fired in 2002 for what was described as "lavish spending" on top of her $2.2 million annual compensation.

So there you have it. Former Hydro One CEO Tom Parkinson was criticized for his expense account irregularities and accepted $3 million in severance when he "resigned." (See Chapter 4's section on David Dingwall and Christiane Ouimet for the public sector definition of "resigned.") Ontario Power Generation CEO Hankinson saw his income grow from $1.6 million a year in 2006 to $2.1 million in 2009, a 31 per cent raise over three years. No wonder the union employees are squawking about 6 per cent over two years.

Oh yes, and former Energy Minister Dwight Duncan? We guess he did such a great job on the finances of Ontario's Ministry of Energy that the Liberals made him finance minister for the whole province. In November 2010 he announced a 10 per cent cut in hydro bills, a move that will cost the government $1 billion each year for the next five years. That would be taking $1 billion out of your left pocket and putting it into your right pocket. After borrowing it from someone else, of course, since Ontario has a $200-billion debt already. Did we mention that somewhere?

And this brings us to Eleanor Clitheroe, one of history's great examples of abuse of entitlement. Clitheroe, like so many of our government appointees to juicy jobs, came to her public sector career opportunity by way of politics. She was Ontario's Deputy Minister of Finance from 1990 to1993 under the NDP government of Bob Rae. She then became a vice-president at Ontario Hydro, and served as president and CEO when the corporation's name was changed to Hydro One. In 2002 she was named Business Woman of the Year by the *National Post*, but soon afterward was fired as Hydro One's CEO after a public controversy arose regarding her substantial salary and benefits, including allegations that Hydro One paid $40,000 for reno-vations to Clitheroe's Toronto home, and that her children were shuttled about by limousine at taxpayers' expense.[18] Clitheroe earned a base salary of $741,000 in 1999, $1.4 million in 2000, $1.7 million in 2001, and $1.5 million in 2002. In 2001, her last full year of work at Hydro One, she took home more than $2.2 million, including $174,000 for a car and $172,000 for vacations.[19] This takes the terms "vacation pay" and "company car" to a whole new level.

You might think that if you're making $2 million in salary you could pay for your own home renovations and child care, but that's the whole problem of trying to run the public sector like a business. Business people are notorious for trying to maximize their wealth. That's why they go into business—because it offers the opportunity for unlimited wealth should they be successful. In business there are checks and balances to channel that greed into productive work and protect shareholders. In the public sector, by the time the auditors or the media or the public discovers how they've been ripped off, the deed is done. In business, if you get caught stealing from the company you are either forced to make restitution, you are fired, or you go to jail. In the public sector, if you get caught with your hand in the cookie jar—no, make that your wheelbarrow in the vault—you get a massive severance package and a fat pension for life. And then you are replaced by somebody with equally questionable ethics.

Clitheroe takes the cake, though. After being fired she was given a pen-sion of $25,637.08 a month (yes, a month). She then sued the government and requested that her pension be raised to $33,644.21[20] a month—slightly more than the average Hydro One pensioner gets annually, and almost five times the average annual CPP payment.

In the lawsuit, which was finally dismissed by the Ontario Court of Appeal in 2011, her lawyer noted that Clitheroe is the "sole breadwinner" for a family of four, and that she was supporting an ailing relative. Aren't we all sister, aren't we all. Clitheroe was indeed scheduled to receive the higher pension amount based on her negotiated contract with the government, which gave her two years of pension accrual for every one year that she actually worked. We're not making this up! This arrangement started when she was the deputy finance minister in 1992, and she negotiated the same deal with Hydro in 1993 as its chief financial officer. That's on top of payments Hydro employees receive through their registered pension plan, and in addition to supplementary top-up payments. In 2002, before Clitheroe was fired, the Ontario government passed legislation limiting the pension plans of its executive employees. Before the pension lawsuit, she had lost a $30-million suit against the government for slander and false dismissal, and before that was denied a $6-million severance that she was originally due to receive. Today she can be found working as an Anglican priest and assistant curate at St. Cuthbert's, a church in Oakville, Ontario. She is known to her parishioners as "Reverend Ellie."

6

EDUCATION

The New Sacred Cow

*The more that learn to read the less learn how to make a living.
That's one thing about a little education. It spoils you for actual
work. The more you know the more you think somebody owes you
a living.*

Will Rogers

This has been a lot of fun thus far, so let's take a look at a few more
examples to give you a better understanding of the style and substance of
the commitments that have been made on your behalf for the future well-
being of your public sector employees. We've already discussed one of
the most notable public pensions (the Ontario Teachers' Pension Plan),
but let's look at the rest of the education system to see if everyone in it
is as lucky as Ontario teachers. Naturally we all hope that our educators
are much smarter than the rest of us; after all, we are entrusting our children to their care, and children represent our hope for the future of our
country. We also hope teachers are instilling sound moral principles in
our kids through leadership. So let's see how the people at the top of the
education pyramid are modeling good citizenship and career-planning on
our behalf.

Feathers were ruffled in the ivory towers in 2009 when the University of Calgary was forced to reveal their retirement package for outgoing university president Harvey Weingarten: $4.75 million.[1] The university had successfully hidden the value of Weingarten's package for several years, a move that has triggered an investigation by the auditor general's department.

The chair of the university's board of governors suggested the omission was merely a record-keeping oversight that has since been corrected. The amounts have not changed, however.

"It was a miscommunication between what the obligation that had been incurred in relation to the pension was and the reflection of the same by the financial people and the financial statements," said the board chair, Jack Perraton.

The president of the faculty association was not impressed by the board's efforts to transfer focus from the amount to the "recording" of the amount. "The issue is proportion," said Anne Stalker. "Let's have the right proportion between the president's benefits and faculty member's benefits and staff at the rest of the university."

The auditor general investigated the oversight and says it is now properly accounted for on the university's financial statements. Whew! That's a relief. We are sure the graduating students of the U of C leaving the campus with their staggering student loan encumbrances will be satisfied that proper accounting has now taken place!

Mr. Weingarten's story illustrates three interesting aspects of pension funding in the public sector. First, of course, is the rather amazing sum of almost $5 million as a retirement gift. When you consider that the average RRSP value of Canadians is only $25,000, you can see how big the gap is between the lifestyle our top civil servants will have in retirement compared to the one an average Canadian can look forward to.

Of course, Canadians have their CPP payouts—an average of $6,148 in 2011. But Mr. Weingarten also receives that. News reports pointed out that the $4.75 million is not a lump sum, and will be paid out over the course of his lifetime. Based on a final salary of $441,000 at 70 per cent, that would be $308,000 per year. Either way, payments start right away. Mr. Weingarten retired at 54.

The second point is the lack of transparency regarding the way our tax dollars are being awarded in contract negotiations. This pension payout only became public knowledge when Weingarten retired, even though he had been employed at the University of Calgary (U of C) for nine years, and the commitment was made to entice him to leave a much lower-paying position at McMaster University. Even the statement of responsibility from the chairman of the board of the university shows a lack of clarity. Can you understand what he is talking about?

"It was a miscommunication between what the obligation that had been incurred in relation to the pension was and the reflection of the same by the financial people and the financial statements," said board chair Jack Perraton.

A miscommunication between "obligation" and "reflection." Apparently "obligation" and "reflection" are the names of two staffers in the financial department at the U of C. We hate to criticize the head of one of our leading educational institutes, but this statement is clearly an attempt to spin the problem and hope it goes away, rather than a clear admission of responsibility.

As the U of C's student newspaper, *The Gauntlet,* points out, this "mis-communication" changes the president's "non-cash benefits" (pension, supplemental pension, health care, dental care, life insurance, short- and long-term disability insurance, rent-free upscale house, etc.) from $180,000 per year, as previously reported, to $347,000.[2] This amounts to $1.5 million over nine years. No problem, says Mr. Perraton, we're just not very good at math here at the U of C—I'll just fix that right now with a couple of keystrokes!

The third point to understand is how Weingarten and Perraton con-spired to tweak the system and give Weingarten more than he was entitled to. Further research by angry students and faculty who had faced years of increased tuition fees and staff cuts under Weingarten's management (in July 2009, Weingarten announced 200 job cuts to the U of C busi-ness unit[3] to begin in the fall, citing a $14-million deficit at the institute) showed that the university signed a statement of principles in 2007 to credit Mr. Weingarten with 22 years of past service with his previous employer, McMaster University in Hamilton.[4] This was more than 6½ years after he was hired in Calgary. The statement of principles was noted in the 2009 financial statements.

Perraton's oversight became public knowledge in 2009, but the deci-sion to merge Weinberg's two pensionable earnings periods was actually made before he was hired. Apparently the president's salary of $269,000 and benefits package of $180,000 was not enough to entice him to leave McMaster. Perraton described the circumstances in 2001 as "fair and reasonable to attract a very talented individual to the university."[5]

Also not revealed until later was the fact that McMaster will contribute nothing to the pension; the entire amount will come from the University of Calgary's budget. So, in fact, the U of C relieved McMaster of its pension liability to Weingarten. Of course, at the end of the day it's all taxpayers' money, and with the nationwide portability of pensions, who can keep track anymore.

The Gauntlet further revealed that Weingarten's salary had grown from $269,000 in 2002 to $441,000 in 2009—a 64 per cent increase over seven years. Under Weingarten's management, executive pay for his senior staff jumped from $859,000 to $2.15 million—an increase of 150 per cent, and executive benefits totaled an additional $2.78 million.

Perraton called it fair compensation, noting that Weingarten would have received a higher salary and pension if he were in the private sector.

This often-touted idea that public sector employees would all receive more money were they working in the private sector is totally unfounded and, in fact, quite ridiculous. The suggestion that private industry would be lining up to pay Mr. Weingarten a compensation package in the range of $750,000 a year (its true value when salary, benefits, and pension are combined) is ludicrous. Weingarten's degrees include a bachelor of science, a master of science, a master of philosophy, and a doctor of philosophy (Ph.D.). There are hundreds, if not thousands, of people with equivalent qualifications. He has no business degrees whatsoever and his entire career path has prepared him to do nothing except work in the field of education. Had he decided to pursue a career in science he would have been hard-pressed to break six figures. According to Payscale.com, a research scientist can expect to make between $41,000 and $89,000 a year in Canada's private sector.

Calgary's enticement to Weingarten, in effect, turned the nine years of pensionable income for which the U of C would have been obligated into 31 years of pensionable income. More importantly for the financial calculations, it is common practice for public sector pensions to be based on the last five years of income (i.e., the highest possible amount, rather than the average amount over a working career). Had those two pensions remained separate, his 22-year Ontario pension would have been based on his final five years of income as a professor at McMaster; his Alberta pension, based on a much higher income as president of the University of Calgary, would have only been multiplied by a factor of nine. By combining the two he was eligible to have his pension based on his final five years of higher income at Alberta multiplied by a 31-year factor, resulting in a much higher payout. Read on for the details.

Suppose these were two separate pensions, as there would be in the private sector if Weingarten had moved from one private school to another. A 2 per cent-accrual rate and a salary of $169,000 from McMaster after 22 years would have entitled him to a pension of around $75,000 a year. Nine years at Calgary with a top salary of $441,000 would have added $80,000 per year, for a total of $155,000. However, the portability option combines the qualifying years and allows the final five years to be used as a base, resulting in an estimated $308,000 a year—a $2.78-million retirement bonus paid for by higher tuitions and higher taxes.

Portability is a special rule that applies to the public sector. Can you imagine someone going to work at Ford, for example, and saying, "I just left Chrysler with 15 years of service and I expect you will pay me for the pensions I accrued there." Portability does not apply in the private sector and is an example of the special rules afforded public sector employees, all paid for by taxpayers.

You might think that since Weingarten transferred from one university to another it would be natural to combine one pension with the other. In reality, education is a provincial concern and funded separately by the taxpayers of the individual provinces, so there is no legal reason why the two employments should be combined. Had they remained separate, taxpayers would have saved money, but as we can see, saving taxpayers money is not a significant concern for people at the top of the education pyramid. Maximizing their own compensation, benefits, and retirement packages is a significant concern, however.

The response from students and faculty at the university was near universal in its condemnation of both the principle and the practice as demonstrated by the board and executive. Alberta Union of Public Employees

Local 52 chairwoman, Shirley Maki, said she was "shocked and dismayed at the dollar amount in this time of economic rough times [*sic*]. To have one person who is able to receive that kind of money taken out of a budget that is struggling to make ends meet feels very wrong."[6]

When Weingarten announced the 200 job cuts he explained that "we are required to live within our means and that's what we are trying to do." Apparently he was not using the royal "we," and therefore living within means did not apply to him.

The university's Students' Union president, Charlotte Kingston, said $4.75 million is a huge number to swallow, especially when many students are struggling to pay their tuition. Kingston said Weingarten's pension is part of a bigger problem. "We can make a huge deal just around pension money, but really the issue is how much we're paying all our executives," she said. "Obviously the president is not the only one making a huge salary and expecting a huge pension. We have a whole team of senior administrators making hundreds of thousands a year and their pensions will reflect that salary."[7]

The faculty association at the University of Calgary, in the October 2009 issue of the *Canadian Association of University Teachers Bulletin*, called on the administration to scale back what it calls an "obscene" supplementary-pension deal for outgoing university president Harvey Weingarten. "One of our big concerns with the auditor general's report is his suggestion that there is nothing wrong with the amount the president is receiving," said faculty association president, Anne Stalker. The faculty association suggests the amount is "additional under-the-counter benefits dressed up to look like a pension."

"This has a significant financial impact on the university," said Stalker. "It will be like we are paying two presidents, while at the same time staff are being laid off, academic staff vacancies are not being filled, and some departments can't afford to buy pens."[8]

More likely the university will be paying for four presidents, since three former presidents are still alive, plus the one actually working. Yes, early retirement is a wonderful thing if you are in the bell jar.

So did the good doctor buy a house on the beach somewhere, get out the rocking chair, maybe write his memoirs? Of course not. He got another job—in the public sector, where he can start building yet another pension.

On July 1, 2010, Dr. Harvey P. Weingarten became president and CEO of the Higher Education Quality Council of Ontario.

Is Calgary an Aberration?

You might be hoping that the situation at the University of Calgary is merely an aberration and doesn't reflect the norm at the many universities and colleges across the country. Unfortunately, this is not the case. Public sector contracts, both unionized and non-unionized, use a process called benchmarking, in which settlements awarded in one location are used as a template for other locations. We will see better examples of this in the next chapter when we discuss police compensation.

Calgary's stunning display of largesse is equaled across the country. Let's take a look at McMaster University in Hamilton, the very same university that was spared millions of dollars by Calgary's generosity. In 2008 Peter George was the highest paid university president in Ontario, with total income and taxable benefits of $533,900.[9] Naturally he had all the bells and whistles possible in his contract, including two life-insurance policies, $30,000 over the five-year contract for "financial estate planning, including legal counsel, in respect of his personal affairs," memberships in local clubs, a nearly $11,000-per-year car allowance (which is declared as a taxable benefit in his yearly salary disclosure), a $20,000-a-year "Health Care Spending Account" to be used for expenses not covered by the university's regular staff benefits, and provision for "business-class" air travel on flights longer than four hours. And of course he would be set for life with a pension, estimated to be about $350,000 per year, indexed for inflation.

But there was more.

Hidden from taxpayers was a "golden handshake" worth an additional $1.4 million. The money will be paid over 14 years at a rate of $99,999 a year. Salary disclosure laws require universities to disclose the names of all employees paid $100,000 or more in a calendar year. If George were paid one dollar more each year after retirement, the university would have been required to report it publicly. McMaster spent two years—and $66,000 of your money in legal fees—to try to prevent the Hamilton Spectator and the general public from gaining access to the agreement.

So to summarize: Despite Peter George being the highest-paid university president in Ontario, McMaster's board of directors felt it necessary to provide him a "secret" retirement benefit of $1,399,986[10] spread over 14 years to be paid AFTER he was no longer working for them. In a Hamilton Spectator article from March 2010,[11] Dr. George said he now considers attempting to hide the retirement bonus from disclosure to be "the most foolish thing he did in office." According to Dr. George, he takes "full responsibility for the stupidity of converting [his] post-retirement allowances into a figure that was seen quite clearly as an attempt to avoid public disclosure." However, he didn't offer to return any of it. And apparently none of the university's board members saw any foolishness in it:

Naturally this would be a one-time exemption from common sense and financial responsibility, right? Wrong again, taxpayer. McMaster Vice-President John Kelton is estimated to be receiving an even higher payout—up to $1.44 million—when his contract expires on June 30, 2011.[12]

So that's the University of Calgary and McMaster University. Surely the rest of our campuses—which are chronically short of cash and have continually raised tuition, creating an entire generation of educated graduates saddled with crippling student loans, and at the same time an entire generation of handsomely-rewarded retired professors and administrators—have done a better job?

Sadly, no. After all, they have to compete with U of C and McMaster for the few super-talented administrators who would otherwise all be running McMaster (or U of C), or working in private industry and making far more—if anyone still believes that nonsense. We think this band of elites will be happy to stay in the ivory tower, where they have lifetime security, comfortable hours, and these kinds of salaries:

- David Johnston, president of the University of Waterloo, total compensation in 2010 of $1,041,881.[13]
- University of Alberta president Indira Samarasekera had a good year in 2009–10 earning $936,000 in compensation and benefits and struck a deal with the university to buy her house for $930,000.[14]

- In 2009 Tina Dacin, director of corporate social responsibility at Queen's School of Business, was paid over $475,000 including benefits.[15]
- Thirteen other Ontario university employees were compensated more than $400,000 in 2008, with another 59 clearing the $300,000 hurdle.[16]

Ontario-wide, 10,461 university employees made the $100,000-plus list. The grand compensation total of post-secondary institution employees on the Sunshine List is $1.4 billion, and that's just Ontario universities. The total number of Sunshiners[17]—the total of all government employees in Ontario on the list in 2010—was 71,478. Using the 70 per cent-of-income rule, this will lead to a pension payout of $980 million per year when these employees are retired. And you will be paying $1.4 billion for their replacements—actually, you will be paying more in both cases, since pensions are protected from erosion by cost-of-living indexing, and compensation inducements continue to escalate.

Clearly Peter George was well-suited for his career path. But the question remains, what is it worth to the taxpayers of Ontario? Is Peter George worth almost twice as much as the prime minister of Canada, who was paid $317,574 in 2010? More than three times the premier of Ontario, who was paid $209,000? And what of the trickle-down effect? The president's salary effectively sets the top of the pyramid and is the benchmark by which all lower salaries for university employees are measured. And as mentioned earlier in this chapter, while Mr. Weingarten's salary increased 64 per cent over seven years, the compensation for his senior staff increased by 150 per cent.

University Pensions

So if universities are short of cash for operating, what about their pension plans? Have they at least set aside enough money to take care of their employees' retirements? Remember that these are the smartest people in Canada, so surely they have been able to arrange suitable funding for their own pensions.

Unfortunately that turns out not to be the case. The university pensions, like so many other public sector pensions, are underfunded and have future liabilities that will need to be picked up by the public purse—meaning you. Let's take a look at where these problems come from.

Like so many of our pension plans, fund managers are super-optimistic about the rate of return considering the inconsistency of stock markets over the past two decades. The university plans are based on a 6.5 per cent rate of return in order to fund the plans. But, as we have mentioned throughout the book—volatility has become the norm.

Because these high expectations of interest rates have not been met, contributions by employees are too low to support the payments that have been committed to retirees. This again puts an unfair burden on the taxpayer, who not only pays the "employer" portion of contributions, but will also have to pay the shortfall. In 2009–10 at McMaster University, pension plan contributions consisted of $47.3 million from taxpayers and $15.2 million from employees, a 75–25 split. The McMaster pension funds had a shortfall of $375.4 million.[18] At the end of fiscal 2009/2010, the University of Guelph had deficits in its pension plan in the amount of $344 million. As well they had an additional $221.5 million accrued liability for non-pension post-employment benefits (OPEBs). An internal budget document stated that "post-employment expenses and liabilities are currently the greatest risk to the University's long-term financial viability."[19]

This information is readily available to taxpayers and employees, and is certainly well understood by the pension fund managers, but the problem is simply being ignored. McMaster's 2009 annual financial report showed that the university was short by $375.4 million in its pension fund. We are sure this won't surprise you by now, but it's interesting to note that the highest-paid employee at the University of Toronto in 2008 was not in fact the president, but rather the managing director of investment strategy. John Lyon's total compensation was $557,474.[20] This was the same year that the University of Toronto Asset Management Fund he was responsible for lost $1.3 billion. Wonder what he gets in a good year?

Let's not Forget the School Boards

In addition to the dozens of universities and colleges, and of course the tens of thousands of teachers in Canada, we also have a significant number of management positions within our school systems. Those in management have not been idle in lining up for some pretty outrageous taxpayer handouts. In particular they seem to have mastered the art of being paid to leave, even when it's by their own choice. Take a look at some of these numbers from British Columbia.

Brian Bastien, a former associate superintendent in the Surrey school district, received total compensation worth $614,382 in 2009–2010. Bastien's base salary was $117,095 but he received $486,650 in "vehicle allowance, unused vacation, retiring allowance, and severance payout," according to the school board's own statement. The district used privacy laws to avoid explaining the dismissal beyond saying it was "without cause" so they were obligated to pay him severance.[21]

Mark Lee topped Bastien however, receiving a severance/compensation package of $252,287—including his base salary of $117,261 from the Abbotsford district. Bastien worked eight years to get his severance, but Lee picked up his pot of gold just 10 months after he accepted the job. The district never explained why Lee left either. Hey, who needs a reason?

Supervisory jobs in the B.C. education system are pretty lucrative even if you have to stay around and put in the time. Bryan Ennis in Stikine, a district with only 260 students, received compensation of $171,088, including a salary of $129,064. The next smallest district, Central Coast with only 270 students, paid its superintendent, Denise Perry, a salary of $142,236, a bonus of $648, and other benefits that brought the total to $176,209.

That's right, Mr. Ennis and Ms. Perry were paid more than $650 per student. If each classroom had 25 students there would be 11 teachers and maybe a principal to supervise? It makes you wonder what Ennis and Perry were doing with their time to justify $170,000.

Will it get better or worse in the future? Do you need to ask? Education spending in 2010 in Ontario was budgeted at $21.4 billion. In April 2011, the Ontario Teachers' Pension Plan reported a record investment return of $13.3 billion, or 14.3 per cent. Did this solve its deficit? No. Despite ending 2010 with $107.5 billion in assets, the fund is still short $17.2 billion.[22,23] The report notes that teachers are living longer than expected, with more than 90 members over the age of 100.

Nova Scotia School Boards Face Budget Cuts

The challenge facing school boards across the country is that the future will inevitably include budget cuts, and they have no plan to rebuild our education system using a more economical model. The major part of the problem is that salaries and benefits continue to escalate faster than the economy, making them a larger percentage of the overall budget every year, leaving less and less for the rising hard costs of education such as building maintenance, higher electricity, and fuel costs. Nova Scotia, facing this reality, announced for 2010 that its school boards were facing cuts of $196 million over three years, up to 22 per cent of the total budget.[24] Educators have said the cuts could result in province-wide losses of 70 small schools, 300 bus drivers and janitors, 600 teachers' assistants and student workers, and up to 2,000 classroom teachers. In a culture used to continual increases, an actual budget cut is incomprehensible. In the City of Halifax, over 80 per cent of the school board budget went toward employee compensation.

"It's huge. No increase, for a school board, is a cut," said Trudy Thompson, chair of the Chignecto-Central Regional School Board. "Now we're cutting 22 per cent over three years? It's just unbelievable."[25]

Nova Scotia has 35,000 fewer students than it did a decade ago, but the education system is now more expensive for taxpayers. School boards responded by reviewing their programs and identifying 820 unnecessary positions and offering an additional $200 million in savings. Just kidding. Boards responded, as usual, by urging parents to pressure the government and threatening that their kids would be left years behind the times if the cuts go through.

"Students across our board will have less supports," Superintendent Gary Clarke said. "They'll have less options in terms of the programming that they can receive. They'll have larger class sizes. I'd be questioning whether or not the education system will meet the needs of my child, and that's a very serious thing," Clarke said.[26] This reaction is common throughout the public sector. "Just leave us alone so we can get bigger and bigger. Money? That's your problem, don't make it mine."

In Canada there are various issues known as the third rails of politics. The expression is in reference to the rail on an electric train track that carries a high-voltage electrical charge. Wikipedia describes a third rail as:

[A] metaphor in politics to denote an idea or topic that is so "charged" and "untouchable" that any politician or public official who dares to broach the subject would invariably suffer politically.

In Canada these third-rail issues have traditionally been policing, education, and health care. Now the issue of compensation and pensions has become a third rail, integrated together to create a very safe situation for the protected class, those inside the bell jar.

In 2011 StatsCan published an annual report called Education Indicators.[27] The report showed that enrollment in elementary and secondary schools across Canada dropped from 5 million in 2001–2002 to 4.7 million in 2008–2009. The total drop was 6 per cent.[28]

Taxpayers might have expected staff levels to likewise drop 6 per cent, but this was not the case. Full-time equivalent educators increased from 316,574 to 338,361, or by 7.2 per cent.[29] The "full-time equivalent educators" category takes part-time teachers and adds them together to calculate full-time teacher positions.

StatsCan should include the total spending on education in its report but does not. Let us provide the example of Alberta as representative of all provinces. In 2002–2003, operating expenses for K–12 education (kindergarten through twelfth grade) were $3.8 billion. By 2011 the same expenses were $6.0 billion, almost double.[30] The number of teachers rose from 29,967 to 32,797, an increase of 9.4 per cent over the same period, while student enrollment had increased from 549,923 to 564,617, an increase of only 3 per cent. Spending went from $6,939 per student to $10,743. Either our kids are 54 per cent smarter or our teachers are 54 per cent richer.

Combine a couple of third-rail issues like public sector compensation and education, health care, or policing, and you will find politicians hightailing in the other direction as fast as they can. It is impossible for them to address pensions and their related costs when they have the best pensions of all.

7

POLICE PENSIONS

Every society gets the kind of criminal it deserves. What is equally true is that every community gets the kind of law enforcement it insists on.
Robert Kennedy

When we take a closer look at the history of police contract negotiations, we find some very strange logic being used to support the ever-increasing salaries of our employees. It has become standard practice amongst all police forces across the country to compare their salary with salaries being paid to police departments in other jurisdictions. This is known as bench-marking, and has been accepted by arbitrators and negotiators as a basis for justifying their decisions in awarding increasingly generous contracts. However, there is absolutely no basis of fact to support the idea that a police officer in Saskatoon, for instance, should receive the same salary, benefits, and pension plan as a police officer in Halifax. Or that police officers in all cities should consistently receive the same cost-of-living increases, and that these increases should be higher than the real rate of inflation. There are many other potential criteria that could be applied to police compensation that would be more relevant.

For instance, would it not make more sense that police officers in high-crime areas should receive more money, since we might assume that they face a higher risk of personal injury? Police forces often justify higher salaries by pointing to low crime rates as a reflection of the great job they are doing. There are some very real problems with this kind of argument, not the least of which is that it is totally insulting to police officers in higher crime areas.

Consider this quote from Halton Regional Police Chief Cary Crowell: "We want to make sure officers in Halton remain comparable with other police services. I wouldn't want our officers to earn significantly less. Our officers deserve no less than those in other police services."

Halton Region is composed of Burlington, Halton Hills, Milton, and Oakville and has been ranked as the safest regional municipality in Canada for the past three years, according to *Maclean's* magazine. Halton's officers received a 9 per cent increase in salary (3 per cent per year) in their last three-year contract, but their overall department budget increase will be in the range of 6–7 per cent annually, largely because of the true cost of wage settlements. Halton has 627 uniformed officers, and a first-class police constable earns $83,274 a year. There was one murder in Halton in 2009, and two attempted murders. Halton Police Association president Duncan Foot defended the high salaries, saying "that salary is to attract those higher-qualified applicants. Halton routinely recruits some of the best and brightest police and candidates in the province."[1]

Here's the problem with that logic: If all the brightest and best police and candidates in the province work for Halton, what does that say about the calibre of the police in the rest of the province? Is Mr. Foot suggesting that police officers everywhere else are inferior to those in Halton?

The Ontario Provincial Police Association (OPPA) negotiated a new contract in 2010 and apparently accepted the Ontario government's request for a pay freeze. However, before it accepted "no increases" in 2012 and 2013, the OPPA negotiated a 5.08 per cent increase in 2011 for its 8,400 members, plus a guarantee that Ontario Provincial Police (OPP) will be the province's highest-paid force by 2014. So the association's public stance of "no pay increase" was all smoke and mirrors.

Karl Walsh, the OPPA's president, said the deal puts the OPP on par with York Regional Police (in Ontario's Municipality of York), and that it still represents "real restraint." During the OPP's last round of bargaining, he said, officers received smaller increases than their peers. "We fell from our traditional standing in the policing community of being number one down to number seventeen," he said. "So there had to be some levelling of the playing field."

So the OPP, which dropped from being number one to number 17 in pay, will be going back to number one in 2014. What do you think the unions representing those forces that previously ranked one to 16 will be looking to do when their contracts come up for renegotiation? It seems that "some levelling of the playing field"—another term for benchmarking— means leap-frogging over everyone else's level to reach the highest level yet attained by anyone (or even higher) if you have to be Number One.

The insulting part of all of this is that every spokesperson is saying that his officers are better than all other officers and, even more to the point, implying that his officers would do a lesser job if they were paid less. They are also suggesting that all of the best police officers would flock to the municipality that pays the highest salary, which is ridiculous.

Let's assume, for instance, that Saskatoon decided to pay its officers $10,000 a year more than any other force in Canada. Would all of the best police officers in Canada uproot their families and leave the communities they live in to make an extra $10,000? The question is actually moot, because when they get to Saskatoon they will discover no available positions because the city's police officers have a lifetime contract and can only be fired or replaced if found guilty of immoral or illegal conduct. This is unlike private sector jobs where it is expected the current generation Y (ages 18–29) will change jobs 8.3 times over the course of their working lives.[2] So the truth is we don't really have to pay police officers more money in order to keep the "best and the brightest" right where they are, which, as we know by listening to police associations, is everywhere these officers already work, since they just take turns being the highest-paid force in the country, based on who got the last contract settlement. Got it?

In the early summer of 2011, Toronto police got a whopping 11.5 per cent increase over four years. This from the new mayor of Toronto, Rob Ford, who campaigned on a promise to control city spending! This was on the back of a similar contract for the Ontario Provincial Police, who had recently negotiated a new contract. Toronto claimed parity with the OPP to justify the deal. Both these contracts were negotiated during the so-called public sector–wage freeze requested by Liberal leader Dalton McGuinty.

The true cost of the new wage deal for Toronto's police officers is much higher than reported. The raise for police in the new city contract brings salaries for officers to $83,800 per year (an increase of $8,800, up from $75,000).[3] This will generate an extra $6,100 in annual pensions for fully-qualified officers based on the 70 per cent equation.

Police officers are eligible for full pensions as early as age 50. Most will collect these pensions, including the surviving spouse benefit, for 35 years. This boost gives them an additional estimated extra $215,000 in lifetime pensions. Actually, the final figure will be higher because most officers will have higher incomes at retirement, based on a graduated salary grid. Considering there are 5,600 Toronto officers and another 5,600 with the OPP, this 11.5 per cent wage increase means an extra $2.4 billion paid out in lifetime pensions.

To be fair, officers are required to pay half of their required pension contributions. So the base cost to taxpayers is $1.2 billion. However, this is a retroactive pension boost which rewards past service—despite those past contracts already having (lower) pension commitments. These are overruled by the new, richer funding formula. So, many officers will pay only four or five years of extra contributions—or less than $30,000—for their extra $215,000 in pension income. The shortfall will be added to the OMERS current $9-billion ($4.5 billion after smoothing) shortfall.[4] Police in this range will be entitled to about $2 million each in lifetime pensions.

The Toronto Police Services Board was reported in *The Toronto Star* as being very pleased with the deal. Toronto and Ontario taxpayers will not be as pleased when the bill comes due.

Here are some more pertinent questions. If a 10 per cent salary cut for all police officers in Canada was negotiated, do you believe that they would perform their jobs more poorly? Are their standards of job performance completely driven by how much money we pay them? If we paid them $200,000 a year would they become better police officers? We would suggest that the answer in both cases is no, and the implied suggestion that competent police officers can be found only by paying them higher and higher salaries, allowing them to work shorter careers, retire earlier, and receive a 70 per cent-of-income lifetime pension for themselves and a surviving spouse, does not in any way, shape, or form reflect the quality, integrity, and professionalism of our police forces.

It is unacceptable that benchmarking only against other public sector jobs is used for contract negotiations. If the public sector needs to use benchmarking they should benchmark salaries against those in the private sector. Compensation settlements should be based on a much broader range of factors, such as crime rate and the long-term sustainability of city or provincial finances. Cities get hammered by arbitration as well. City police forces are paid by the city, but if they are not happy they'll go to provincial arbitration. Most police forces across Canada have seen crime rates fall dramatically, by between 15 and 30 per cent, across the country. Yet, of course, compensation packages have skyrocketed. The long-term trend of lower crime rates will continue because aging baby boomers with walkers and wheelchairs don't commit many crimes.

How much policing can we afford? What is fair to both them and us? Let's look at some examples of police compensation and you can decide for yourself if our policing costs have gotten out of hand.

Toronto Police Force Salary and Benefits

As you have seen, the top police forces in the country pay their first-class (highest-ranking) constables over $80,000 per year. In Toronto in 2010 there were 2,159 police service employees on the Sunshine List, but keep in mind this is only base salary. *Toronto Sun* columnist Joe Warmington, an outspoken critic of government over-compensation, said, "Could you be so fortunate to have your child grow up to earn Glen Mackey money? In 2010 he brought home $175,135.25. What is he a doctor? A lawyer? No, Glen Augustine Mackey is a Toronto Police constable. You read it right—175,000 smackers."[5]

Police officers receive far more than their base salary. We turn to the Toronto Police Service's own website to discover the following chart showing that officers' salaries range from $50,000 for a cadet in training to over $81,000 for a first-class constable.

Toronto Police Service Base Salaries

Toronto Police Service

cadet in training	$50,558
4th-class constable	$56,731
3rd-class constable	$64,839
2nd-class constable	$72,948
1st-class constable	$81,046

In addition, full-time employees of the Toronto Police Service are entitled to the following compensation and benefits:

- family health plan;
- dental plan;
- life insurance;
- access to employee credit union;
- pension plan (OMERS);
- paid vacation;
- education reimbursement; and
- employee and family assistance program.[6]

These benefits add approximately 35–40 per cent to the value of any given contract, so in reality, a first-class constable is being paid about $113,000 in total compensation. Naturally, sergeants, staff sergeants, inspectors, staff inspectors, staff superintendents, deputy chiefs, and chiefs all get more money. In case you've lost count, that's 12 separate pay levels from cadet to police chief in the salary grid, each one requiring a pay, benefit, and pension increase. Of course, those health benefit programs are top-of-the-line, with all the bells and whistles.

But it doesn't stop there. Overtime is offered to officers based on the seniority rules of the unions. Senior officers are closest to retirement, and in some cities overtime can still be used to create higher levels of pay on which to base pensions, again driving up the true cost. This gaming of the system, as we noted earlier, is called spiking. As a result of spiking some officers will earn pensions close to 100 per cent of base salaries.[7]

Another goodie offered to police is something called "paid duty." This is the use of off-duty police officers to act as security guards around the City of Toronto. Over the years influential police chiefs have actually gotten this windfall added into city bylaws. One bylaw states that any construction within 30 metres of traffic lights requires a supervising officer. The construction company does not have the option of hiring a security guard for $15 per hour, he must hire an off-duty police officer at $65 per hour. It is estimated that city police earn an extra $8 million a year for this duty.[8]

Police officers routinely retire after 30 years of service, but many don't actually stop working. They simply find another job in the public sector while collecting their police pension and free health care benefits until age 65, and begin to build a second pension,[9] so that by the time they do retire, their taxpayer-guaranteed pension can actually amount to more than they made when they were working.

Now you might think, if you watch a lot of TV police shows, that these overtime requirements are necessary because our front-line officers are engaged in lengthy stakeouts, round-the-clock murder investigations, and cross-country fugitive chases. Danger, fear, and constant risk of death or disability are a daily possibility. The stunning truth is that the highest-paid police officers tend to be those who hand out traffic tickets, and are required to attend court proceedings on behalf of the Crown to make sure those parking tickets are enforced.

According to the Ontario Sunshine List, the Toronto Police Service had over 1,300 employees who earned more than $100,000 in 2009—a 30 per cent increase from the year before. The 2010 numbers were much higher, but were inflated because of the security costs of the G20 Summit. Not a bad boost in the face of the greatest economic crisis since the Great Depression. That's almost 20 per cent of the employees at the police force earning over $100,000 per year, each triggering a $70,000 per year pension. It is interesting to note also that only 380 of the 1,329 police employees who broke $100,000 were actually constables on the beat. The remaining 949 weren't actively involved on the street in enforcing the law at all—they were pushing paper, attending meetings, producing budgets, and writing press releases. Apparently the Toronto police force also has to have the country's highest wages, to attract the "best and the brightest."

Here are a couple of examples for you from the Sunshine List: Michael Thompson, who was paid $161,892, and Abdulhameed Virani, who collected $151,042. Both officers more than doubled their salaries in large measure by writing traffic tickets that required them to make frequent court appearances.

Under the Toronto Police Association collective agreement, police officers who attend court as witnesses during a scheduled day off are paid for a minimum of four hours, at 1.5 times their basic wage, even if the appearance lasts 10 minutes. Officers receive three hours of pay at time and a half if they appear in court before a scheduled shift. Apparently court duty for traffic offences is valued higher than on-the-street police work. Truth is stranger than fiction!

In case you are thinking this was a one-time aberration, and that steps are being taken to reduce these overpayments, here are Thompson and Virani's incomes from 2007: Abdulhameed Virani, $153,784; Michael Thompson, $151,028.[10] According to the TPAC (Toronto Police Accountability Coalition,[11] a police watchdog devoted to making police accountable to the public), these two officers were only third-class constables at the time, with a base salary of about $63,000, so their overtime and court pay gave them a boost of about $88,000, or approximately 140 per cent. They also note that one officer made $102,000 in 2007 without working a single day. He was on leave because he had been charged with extortion and obstructing justice, meaning he was not permitted to work—but he was still paid. You might think that with the police being an integral part of the justice system there might be a way to speed up the legal process for officers charged with crimes—both to save tax-payers money and to send a message to police and the public that this type of image-destroying and trust-corroding behaviour will not be tolerated. Not the case. There have been dozens of cases of police officers being paid (and accumulating pension eligibility) while suspended and waiting to be tried in court on criminal charges.

But back to accounting. Using the strange logic of the Police Association, the Toronto Police Service resisted a request by Toronto City Council to reduce its 2010 operating budget by $4.1 million on the basis that this would delay the hiring of new uniformed officers.[12] Apparently no thought was given to the possibility of rearranging schedules so that existing offi-cers would work only regular hours, and the time and a half and double time that were being paid out in overtime benefits could be allocated to the hiring of new full-time officers. Salaries and benefits represent 83 per cent of the Toronto police operating budget each year.

Case Study: Julian Fantino—Leading by Example

Julian Fantino began his career in policing in 1964 when he joined the Metropolitan Toronto Police as an auxiliary police officer. In 1969 he was appointed as a full-time police constable, and was promoted up through the ranks, eventually serving as London's chief of police (1991–1998), as chief of the York Regional Police (1998–2000), and then as Toronto's police chief (2000–2005). He spent one year as Ontario's Commissioner of Emergency Management before returning to police work as the Commissioner of the Ontario Provincial Police, ending in 2010. Fantino's salary as Toronto police chief in 2004 was $209,611.[13] His OPP salary in 2009 was $251,989.[14]

In 2010 Fantino left the OPP to run successfully as the federal Conservative member of parliament for the riding of Vaughan in a by-election on November 29. Despite some 40 years as a law-enforcement officer with a stated goal to "contribute to the prime minister's tough-on-crime agenda," in January 2011 Fantino was named Minister of State for Seniors. With three police pensions totaling more than $100,000 per year, we're not sure his perspectives on senior issues mirror those of most pensioners. Maybe Prime Minister Harper was expecting a revolt from the growing number of seniors who are living near or below the poverty line, while retired politicians and public servants live in comfort and luxury, and wanted the former law enforcement officer on his side. (Author's note: On May 18, 2011, he was moved to his current portfolio of Associate Minister of National Defence.)

You might think that Chief Fantino's 2004 salary of $209,611 would be sufficient to attract a suitably-qualified replacement, probably someone from within the Toronto force who already knew the lay of the land. In fact, the city found a perfect replacement in Bill Blair, the head of detectives for the force. Blair, like Fantino, is a career police officer and has a long history with the Toronto Police Service. The chief's salary would have been a substantial raise for Mr. Blair, but apparently not enough to get him to accept the promotion. Taking Fantino's salary and multiplying it by the annual 3 per cent raise that all of our government servants seem to need (to offset the 2 per cent annual increase in the cost of living) would have taken Chief Blair's salary in 2007 to $229,047. In reality, Blair was paid $261,403 in 2007, an increase of $32,256,[15] or 14 per cent above what Mr. Fantino might have received had he remained as police chief. Of course, Blair's pension will also take a significant leap.

This would be a good place to quickly explain another interesting facet of public sector pensions, in particular in the police sector where there are so many levels of pay that a person can start as a constable at $50,000 a year and end up as chief at $260,000 a year. At each level, the employee pays a percentage of his income into his pension fund. See the chart below for a visual explanation.

If a police officer spent his career as a $50,000-a-year employee, contributing 10.7 per cent into his pension (the current OMERS rate), he would invest $5,350 per year into the police pension fund. After 30 years he would have invested $160,500. He would then receive a pension of $35,000 a year, using a baseline of 70 per cent of income. In real life, that never happens. Let's look at an example whereby the officer progresses after 10 years to first-class constable, then five years as head of detectives, then five as police chief. His average income might increase to $100,000 a year for 10 years, then $200,000 for five years, and culminate at $250,000 for the final five years he works.

In the table below we outline the contributions based on this scenario.

Years worked	Annual salary	Annual pension contribution	Total pension contribution
1–10	$ 50,000	$ 5,350	$ 53,500
11–20	$100,000	$10,700	$107,000
21–25	$200,000	$21,400	$107,000
26–30	$250,000	$26,750	$133,750
Contribution total			$401,250

Years retired	Annual pension income	Total pension paid out
30	$175,000	$5,250,000

Note: This scenario greatly overestimates the amount that would actually have been contributed. It is only in the past year that the contribution rate moved to this level. In the 60s the contribution rates were 5.5 per cent for many years, and then moved to 6.5 per cent and 7 per cent in the mid-80s and 90s. From 1998–2002 there was a contribution holiday during which employees did not have to pay anything.

In this hypothetical example, the chief would have made lifetime contributions of $401,250 and would be entitled to earn a pension of $175,000 per year. On this basis, his pension will be $5.25 million over the next 30 years, and if we index it at 2 per cent for inflation, he will end up collecting over $7 million. If he started with the force at the age of 20, he could retire with his full pension at age 50.

There is a huge gap between what the employee contributes and what he eventually receives through his pension. The gap is covered mainly by taxpayers, but also by future employees who will have to pay increased contributions to cover such "unfunded liabilities." The chief is taking advantage of a system that allows him to receive a pension benefit based on his final five years of service while his lifetime contributions were made from a much lower salary base. Our recommendation is to change pensions to correspond to a career average rather than a final salary. In the UK Hutton Report on pension reform one of the problems identified is "high flyers" unfairly benefiting from taxpayers and future employees. High-income employees pay low pension contributions based on their career average but collect high pension benefits based on the final 3- or 5-year average salary.

Think this is a special deal for the top players only? Think again. Here's a direct example from a 2004 report by the Ontario Municipal Employees Retirement Service (OMERS),[16] one of the country's largest pension plans:

FIGURE 7.1: Value of an OMERS Pension

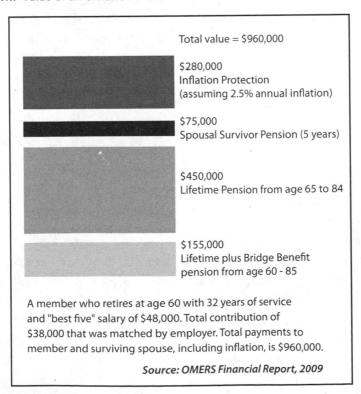

Total value = $960,000

$280,000
Inflation Protection
(assuming 2.5% annual inflation)

$75,000
Spousal Survivor Pension (5 years)

$450,000
Lifetime Pension from age 65 to 84

$155,000
Lifetime plus Bridge Benefit
pension from age 60 - 85

A member who retires at age 60 with 32 years of service and "best five" salary of $48,000. Total contribution of $38,000 that was matched by employer. Total payments to member and surviving spouse, including inflation, is $960,000.

Source: OMERS Financial Report, 2009

As we can see, starting at 70 per cent of best five years salary the first year pension would be $33,600 per year. With a cost-of-living raise of 2.5 per cent each year, this 2004 pensioner would be receiving $39,939 by 2011—an increase of 19 per cent. OMERS lists the total value of the pension as $960,000. With a total contribution of only $38,000, this is a pretty fantastic return on investment, wouldn't you say? And remember, unlike your RRSP investments, this one is guaranteed by your taxes, regardless of what happens in the market. Multiply that by OMERS's 400,000 members and you start to see the size of the problem. Could the OMERS fund ever be short? Is the Pope Catholic? Police in Ontario belong to the OMERS plan, so let's take a look at the plan's current financial situation.

Rising Benefit Obligations

The future cost of pension benefits has been on a dramatic increase for most of the 2000–2010 period. There is no reason to think that the current trend will not continue. The OMERS plan has seen the cost of these benefits obligations increasing annually at 7–9 per cent. At the start of the last decade, the total benefit obligations were in the range of $28 billion. They had escalated to $60 billion by 2010,[17] and future projections show that the cost of the benefit obligation for OMERS will be well in excess of $129 billion.[18] In order to keep up with these obligations, taxpayers will be required to continue funding the OMERS plan at very steep rates.

Virtually ALL public sector pension funds are "underfunded," which is the politically correct way of saying they don't have enough money to meet their obligations. Even after two of the best years for equity investments, with a 10.6 per cent rate of return in 2009 and 12.01 per cent in 2010, these funds are short. More importantly, they are counting on decades of exceptional growth to correct this. Keep your fingers crossed.

The OMERS 2011 financial report states that despite recent high returns its funding deficit has tripled to $4.5 billion as its pension benefit obligations have increased.

The plan requires a 6.5 per cent annual return for the next 15 years to bring itself back into a surplus position by 2025. Will that be a problem? Let's listen to chief financial officer Patrick Crowley.

FIGURE 7.2: OMERS Obligations and Assets

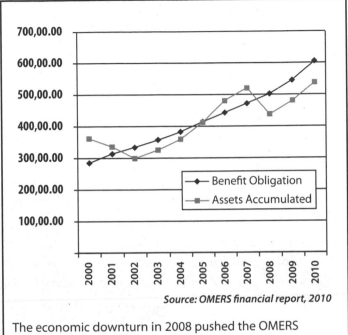

Source: OMERS financial report, 2010

The economic downturn in 2008 pushed the OMERS
pension fund into a deficit position. Fund members
are protected by taxpayer guarantees that essentially
turn public sector pensions into Guaranteed Investments
by putting all of the risk in the hands of taxpayers.

"Based on our asset mix policy and active investment strategy, we
believe we can generate average returns of 7 per cent to 11 per cent annually over the next five years," said Patrick Crowley. "Doing so would return
the plan to surplus between 2015 and 2020—five to 10 years ahead of
schedule."[19]

Note the wildly optimistic predictions of the chief financial officer.
Call your financial advisor and ask her if she can offer guarantees
of 7-11 per cent returns in the next five years. The Ontario Teachers'
Pension Plan has revised its estimates to a 3.15 per cent real rate of return
after inflation[20] in anticipating how much additional tax money it will
need to pay its retirees. Even the CPP is hoping for, at best, a 6 per cent

annual return. Advisors are constantly told never to make predictions on equities because of the volatility of stock markets, and pension experts routinely suggest a safer target for pension funds would be 3 per cent. The total five-year return for the S&P/TSX Composite Index (Standard & Poor's/Toronto Stock Exchange) from July 28, 2006 to July 28, 2011 was 17.7 per cent, or about 3.5 per cent per year.[21] Of course we might expect to hear of Mr. Crowley's retirement long before the surplus target date of 2025, so he will not need to be accountable if his projections are off by a few billion.

As of 2011 there are four former Toronto police chiefs still alive and receiving pensions, and likely many more deputy chiefs and senior staff members, since senior employees often retire shortly after their five years of service at top income are up, thus maximizing their pensions while minimizing their years of employment. Here are the 2008 salaries on which the pensions of some top Toronto police brass will be based when they retire. Chief Bill Blair, $270,052.59; deputy chiefs Kim Derry, Keith Forde, and Anthony Warr, $199,361; and deputy chief Jane Dick, $185,729.81.[22]

This "early out at the top" career path has been going on for some time now, ensuring a brain drain as the "best and the brightest" of the "best and the brightest"—those whose careers are at their peak and would be the best candidates to continue managing our public sector—take early retirement to maximize their pensions while minimizing their contributions. Yet another reason to end early retirement for public sector employees.

In January 2005, for instance, *The Globe and Mail* reported the retirement of Toronto Police Deputy Chief Steven Reesor.[23] After 30 years of service (the minimum time for a full pension), the 51-year-old (at the peak of his career) joined Magna International, the Aurora-based car-parts giant, as an executive. Deputy Chief Reesor leaves behind nine years of experience as deputy chief. His departure coincided with his being overlooked for the police chief position that went to Bill Blair, which sent the message that he had reached his highest position within the force, and likely the highest salary level on which to base his pension. His recorded salary in 2003 was $187,000. Might as well cash out now and go work for the private sector while being paid a pension by the taxpayers. Probably sounds just like your life.

And as for Mr. Fantino, should he survive as an MP for six years he will have qualified for his third public sector pension. He was eligible for one from the Metro Toronto Police Benefit Fund, OMERS, and as a Member of Parliament. To be fair we are not sure that he triggered all of these pensions and this is why we are calling for disclosure of pension funds much like the Sunshine List. Triple-dipping, anyone?

8

HOW MUCH DO YOU REALLY OWE?

Forbes *publishes a list of the world's richest people. Who would it put on its list of the world's poorest? Surely, America's young people would lead the rankings. Each one is shackled to a ball and chain of debt—hammered into place by an older generation—before he even begins to compete. Their parents and grandparents bequeath them public debt and unfunded obligations of more than $200 trillion. It hardly seems fair.*

Bill Bonner, *The Daily Reckoning*

So now that you've had a glimpse of the pension problems facing the majority of Canadians, let's look at how they affect you. How much money do you owe and how do you intend to repay it before you die? We're not talking about your personal debts here, your mortgage, credit cards, line of credit, and bank loans. You may have been very careful with your personal financial planning. Your governments have not been as careful, however. We are talking about your share of the money that the federal, provincial, and municipal governments of Canada have borrowed on your behalf to meet the various commitments that they have decided are worth borrowing for. And also the multiple future commitments these governments have taken on that you have agreed to pay for. Yes, you.

Well, okay, maybe you didn't exactly agree to pay these debts. In fact, we're guessing that you're not really aware of many of these commitments that you are financially responsible for, but the fact remains that you will have to pay your share. Still not getting the picture? Pour yourself a coffee (or maybe a stiff drink would be better), sit down, and let us give you a brief summary.

Federal Government Deficits, Debts, and Commitments

You may be familiar with terms such as "deficit" and "debt," which are often used during the course of budget discussions when the media covers our federal government and its policy-making procedures. Basically it works like this: The federal government decides to implement certain plans such as buying planes or submarines for the military, funding the arts, or making foreign aid donations—or just paying its staff, which is an ever-growing expense. It also transfers funds to the provinces and territories. In 2009, Ottawa transferred $26.9 billion to fund provincial health care.[1] This money comes from taxes. The main source of federal revenue is income tax ($116 billion personal, $29 billion corporate), which accounts for about 65 per cent of the $218 billion in revenue collected in 2010. Most of the remainder comes from consumption taxes, such as those on GST, energy, and duties and excise taxes. The government also collected $17 billion in employment insurance (EI) contributions that year.[2]

In addition to collecting taxes, the government makes future commitments on your behalf. These include promises to fund pensions to government workers, plus the Canada Pension Plan (CPP), Old Age Security (OAS), and the Guaranteed Income Supplement (GIS). This of course is a great idea, because how else could these massive national projects and services be financed if not through the joint contributions of all Canadians? The problem is that our federal government, for most of our lifetime, has run a yearly deficit on its annual plans, meaning that each year it spends more than it collects. This is known as "deficit financing" and is practised by pretty much every government in the Western world. *The Economist's* Global Debt Clock estimates current (August, 2011) total worldwide federal government debt as $40.1 trillion, increasing at about $5 million per minute. The term "deficit," then, is used to describe the annual shortfall— the difference between the money collected each year by our governments and the money spent each year by those governments. The term "net debt," meanwhile, is the running total of all previous unpaid deficits, money spent that we had to borrow. Pension commitments and future health care costs, on the other hand, are known as "long-term liabilities," because the federal government does not have the money set aside to pay these obligations—but they guarantee to pay them when they come due. The combined net debt and the long-term liabilities are known as the gross debt. Guess where this money is going to come from? (Hint—look in the mirror.)

This was not always the case. In past generations, up until the late 1960s, our federal government operated on a cash flow basis (like a business). The government spent only what it raised in taxes, except during emergencies, such as the Great Depression and World War II, or to fund massive nation-building projects such as the Canadian Pacific Railway in the 1800s. Yet, even here, the government quickly repaid the funds it borrowed. After World War II, Canada owed only $8 billion, a figure that changed little until Pierre Trudeau became prime minister.[3]

Mr. Trudeau, who remains the darling of the baby boomer generation and is remembered as one of Canada's greatest leaders, decided it was pragmatic to borrow a little money each year in order to provide us with more services faster—to build Canada as a "just society" a little faster than cash flow could provide. The plan was based on the idea that we could afford this temporary debt, which we generally pay only the interest on, and would pay the balance later when our economy was bigger and generating more tax revenue.

Nobody seemed too concerned about it at the time. After all, we were in the midst of the biggest economic boom in history, so borrowing against our future seemed like a good idea. Besides, it made politicians look good when they could provide more and more services . . . and pay government employees more and more money . . . and promise their staff (and themselves) better and better pensions. This was 1968. It wasn't a problem in 1969. Or in 1970. Or in 1971. We think you get the picture. But by 1975 we owed $54.3 billion in gross debt, and by 1981, $123.5 billion. Trudeau left office in 1984, but by then the policy of promising more and more to attract votes was part of the political process. Brian Mulroney took over and kept up the pace. By 1993, Mulroney's last year as prime minister, we owed $607.2 billion.[4] Truth is, we're not sure that average Canadians really had a clue of what this meant to them in the long-term. Most Canadians today don't really understand this form of government finance either. So let us give you the numbers.

Federal Debt Passes $500 Billion

Canada's federal (net) debt grew steadily between 5 per cent and 10 per cent per year until 1975 when it began to explode; growing for the next 12 years at more than 20 per cent per year. It broke the $100-billion mark in 1981 and the $200-billion mark in 1985. While the growth slowed in 1988, our federal debt continued to climb, breaking $300 billion in 1988, $400 billion 1992, and $500 billion in 1994. It peaked in 1997 at $563 billion.[5]

Over the past decade it had slowly declined to $458 billion in 2008. Now this has all changed. Our federal debt grew by $5.8 billion in 2008–09, by $53.8 billion in 2009–2010 and is expected to grow by $49.2 billion in 2010–2011. Further, it's expected to grow through at least 2014–2015.

Canada's debt re-passed the $500 billion mark at 4:55:46 a.m. on December 2, 2009.

(Courtesy taxpayer.com)[6]

In 2009 we paid $29 billion in interest on net debt.[7] This is more than the federal government transferred to the provinces for health care last year. Just think—if there was no debt interest to pay we could double our federal spending on health care. We repaid no principal. In 2010, the net debt increased by approximately $59.6 billion because of stimulus spending to prop up bankrupt companies such as General Motors, and is expected to increase by an additional $49.2 billion in 2010–2011. By 2011 the federal government had an outstanding gross debt of $883.3 billion.

Okay, let's stop for a minute before you start to glaze over and lose sight of the point here, which probably happens every time you read news reports on this topic. The point is that you owe this money. Yes, you. This federal gross debt amounts to $26,766[8] ($883.3 billion) for *each person* in your family. When can we expect your cheque to cover this?

But wait, it gets better. Federal government debt is only one form of debt—there is also provincial debt. And with those debts included, my friends, the bill jumps to more than $1.2 TRILLION (or roughly $35,000 per person). *The Economist's* Global Debt Clock—an independent third-party appraisal—lists Canada's government debt at $1.234 trillion as of June 2011.

As we mentioned, we generally pay yearly interest on the net debt at current interest rates averaging about 3–4 per cent, which works out to $30–40 billion per year currently. Since 2000–2001 we have paid $383 billion[9] in interest—money that could have gone into services, hospitals, schools, and roads. However, logic suggests that Canada will have to pay this debt back at some point. Can you do that? Did you say your cheque is in the mail?

Now before we go on to the other debts you owe (yes, there are more), we need to make sure you understand a key point: This is your debt, not "the government's" debt. We say that because this gap in understanding is one reason the situation has gotten so far out of hand. The idea held by most Canadians is that the government and its bureaucrats are somehow separate from us. "They" collect taxes and "they" spend taxes and "they" borrow money and "they" are responsible for the debt, and it is "their" problem.

Wrong. Politicians work for you. You "appointed" them through the democratic electoral process and gave them the freedom to borrow on your behalf and spend on your behalf, but eventually YOU will be the one paying this back. Or your children. Or your grandchildren.

Okay, is the picture clear now? The federal government has borrowed money but it will have to collect that money from you in order to pay it back. And that money has been spent. It's gone. And next year the government will be borrowing more, which you will have to pay back some time in the future.

Let's go Provincial

So that's a quick look at the federal situation. Our provincial governments have followed suit, consistently spending more than they can collect and also running massive operating debts. Let's take a look.

The current total of all provincial (including territories) net debt as of 2010 is $388.3 billion,[10] with annual interest payments of $21 billion! The federal government transferred $62 billion to the provinces last year and yet the provincial deficits still increased by $48 billion, so you can see the mess we are in. Leaders in the field are Ontario with a $193.6-billion debt (now officially a "have-not" province which receives billions in federal equalization payments from other provinces each year) and Québec with a $142.8-billion debt. The provinces have not even calculated their gross debt liabilities from healthcare. William Gairdner, a leading government debt watchdog in Canada, estimates that Canada's gross debt is in the range of $2.4 trillion once health care long-term liabilities are estimated.[11]

So whether you live in one of these failing provinces or not, our transfer system guarantees that you will share in the payback. This adds $11,000 to the bill that every man, woman, and child owes. You owe this and will pay it back one way or the other through income taxes, sales taxes, hidden taxes, and in some cases, just plainly outrageous and blatant tax grabs such as the Ontario government health "premium," introduced in 2004. Faced with ever-growing deficits in the health care system, Ontario's Liberals instituted a health tax payable by all taxpayers, but said it wasn't a "tax," it was a "premium," even though it was based on taxable income. Despite the absurdity of the semantics, Liberals today continue to use the term premium. According to the government website, "the Ontario Health Premium is not related to the Employer Health Tax for Ontario. Each year, revenue from the Ontario Health Premium contributes approximately $2.8 billion to the health care system."[12]

Governments are particularly creative when it comes to rearranging taxes to raise more money. They will have to become even more creative in the years to come. The Harmonized Sales Tax is one example of rearranging the deck chairs on the *Titanic* to raise more money from the same victims. Most provinces are moving full speed ahead into casinos, lotteries, and online gambling in an effort to collect more money from the public. How much more can you afford to pay?

Let's not Forget Municipal Debt

Municipalities are prevented by law from borrowing money to finance yearly spending. However they do receive a range of payments from provincial and federal governments to offset some of their costs when faced with a deficit. Their biggest costs, of course, are employee salaries and benefits (which continue to increase faster than the rate of inflation), and pensions. And their pensions are all in deficit.

Municipalities raise the bulk of their income from business and property taxes. Attracting business is a highly competitive activity as cities with a larger business community are in a better position to provide the services Canadians have come to expect. However, as we know, the large manufacturing companies that were the backbone of the Canadian economy in the last century, with their high salaries, huge land requirements, and significant tax contributions, are a thing of the past. The majority of new jobs in the last two decades have been created by small businesses and through self-employment. A large percentage of people today work at home, as opposed to commercial offices or factories, and do not pay commercial property taxes, which are considerably higher than residential taxes. This declining tax base from the manufacturing sector forces the transfer of municipal costs to residents so that property taxes continue to rise at rates higher than other cost-of-living increases. In December 1999 the manufacturing sector in Canada employed 2.32 million workers. By 2011 this had dropped to 1.78 million.[13]

This is particularly significant for the boomers who are moving into retirement age and generally own large homes with big property tax bills. With diminished private sector pensions and escalating property taxes we can expect a massive property shift as boomers are forced to sell their homes because they can no longer afford to live in them.

So even though your municipality can't run a deficit budget it can commit you to significant future expenses to pay the defined benefit pensions and OPEBs that have been negotiated for your city employees and politicians. You can run, but you can't hide.

How much are these municipal pension deficits? Using Hamilton as an example, the average homeowner there is looking at a deficit of about $2,700 that needs to be added to property tax bills. Extrapolate that across the country and you get another $6.5 billion in pension shortfalls. When combined with budget pressures to provide services, these deficits threaten to bankrupt our municipalities, or drain provincial and federal coffers, creating even more deficits, debt, and interest payments.

What Does that all Mean?

Put it all together and it means that every man, woman, and child in Canada owes somewhere between $36,000—the official government number—and $72,000 when all long-term liabilities are estimated.[14] Add spiralling personal debt to the mix (currently at $25,597 per person[15]), and you can see that our entire country is heading off the edge of a cliff with no real hope of maintaining our collective standard of living.

Sooner or later this bill will have to be paid, and the reshuffling of cash and assets will change our society as we know it, creating a new class of haves and have-nots that will rival British society of the 18th and 19th centuries. We will have a new segment of society—the senior's gentry, if you will, of well-to-do retired former civil servants whom former California Governor Arnold Schwarzenegger called the "protected class"[16]—and a huge group of seniors living under or near the poverty line. The effect of this segmentation of our seniors will trickle down to the working middle class, who typically bear the brunt of all taxation.

We are already seeing the effects of our government's financial failings in a middle-class quality-of-life that by all standards is lower than that of our parents. We now have two parents working in virtually every home, and yet personal debts are at an all-time high. Today there are five workers for every pensioner and once the baby boomers are all in their pension years—about 2025—there will be only 2.5 workers for each pensioner. Not only will these workers have to pay for underfunded pensions, they will also have to begin the virtually endless process of retiring our government debts.

FIGURE 8.1: Ratio of Active Members to Retirees

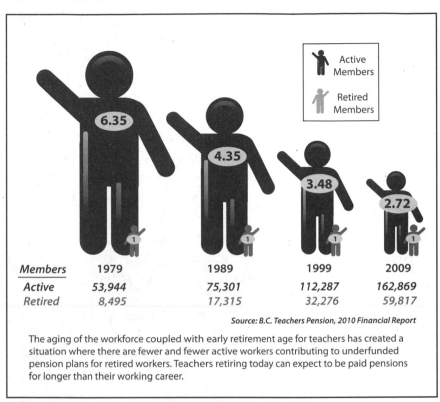

Members	1979	1989	1999	2009
Active	53,944	75,301	112,287	162,869
Retired	8,495	17,315	32,276	59,817

Source: B.C. Teachers Pension, 2010 Financial Report

The aging of the workforce coupled with early retirement age for teachers has created a situation where there are fewer and fewer active workers contributing to underfunded pension plans for retired workers. Teachers retiring today can expect to be paid pensions for longer than their working career.

Can you imagine any way that this equation can work in your favour? If you are up-to-date about current events, you know that every think tank has consistently stated that our health care system can't survive in its current model. And you know that none of our governments can meet the demand for the services we expect.

Perhaps you are one of the lucky ones who have a gold-plated pension, indexed for inflation, and guaranteed by the taxpayers. However, keep this in mind: Our tax system is designed to take from those who have and give to those who don't. This has been wrongly interpreted as a kind of Robin Hood-esque "take from the rich to give to the poor" program, but actually the rich still control their own wealth. They may simply move it offshore where it is not taxable, invest in foreign economies, or just use their lobbying power to create, as they have already, a taxation system that favours their continued accumulation and retention of wealth. The trend of the rich getting richer has been going on for decades. According to StatsCan, the median income of the bottom 20 per cent of Canadians dropped 20.6 per cent from 1980 to 2005, while those in the top 20 per cent increased wealth by 16.4 per cent. The middle 60 per cent stayed almost exactly the same.[17] This is proof that Canada's progressive tax system is not working.

No, we are not likely to become a "tax the wealthy" country. What we might expect, however, is that the increasing group of wealthy middle-class pensioners will face ever-higher taxes, user fees, and clawbacks. Of course that's just speculation. There will be growing political pressure from people who don't have those wonderful pensions and who can only hope that the governments of the future will right this imbalance. On the other hand, since the very people making this decision are beneficiaries of the current situation, would it really, really surprise you if they try everything in their power to leave things the way they are?

We are the first to take an in-depth look at the inequity of our current public sector pension plans. The media, in the future, will be full of reports, studies, and opinions highlighting this disparity and calling out for reform. Yet we expect our governments' answer to this will be to study ways of improving private sector pensions. Indeed, they have no interest in reforming their own pensions downward. Their attitude is "Hey, we're set for life, let's leave that the way it is and see if we can find ways for you guys to save more money for your pensions."

International Story

Some would suggest that the future can't be foretold, but we can predict Canada's future if drastic changes aren't made soon. Canada is on the same path as every other Western country—aging population, low birth rate, diminishing wealth-creating economic sector (the segment of the gross domestic product related to making products rather than providing services), growing public sector with early retirement and substantial pensions, and an unsustainable health care system. Some countries waited too late to make changes and became the canaries in the mine, sending a warning. Some have already heeded the warning and begun the painful changes necessary to restore faith in their ability to manage their economy for the future. Others, such as Canada, remain with their heads in the sand, going along as if nothing is wrong, believing it's business as usual.

This is a collapse that has been building for more than three decades, but the global financial meltdown of 2008 and the steady retirement of the Boomers have caused many people to take a longer-term view and question the sustainability of our economic model. With so many eyes turned to the financial world, it didn't take long for some people to realize that not only were the banks fallible, but our Western economies are also built on false pretenses. The current focus on public debt levels worldwide, early retirement of the public sector, and the constant deficit financing of government services have triggered a wave of crisis that has yet to seriously hit our shores—in the form of government cutbacks, pension defaults, higher borrowing rates, and escalating unemployment—but will very soon if changes are not made.

In 2009 the countries of Iceland, Greece, and Ireland essentially declared bankruptcy. Portugal, Italy, and Spain teeter on the precipice. The United States, Canada, the United Kingdom, and France suffered financial meltdowns of varying degrees, forcing, for the first time in a generation, a serious examination of their governance structures. One of the conditions of the bailout in Ireland was that the country use its pension reserves to finance its spending,[18] an ominous warning to pensioners everywhere. Once the reserves are spent on general government costs, how will they be replaced? Ireland is being pressured to raise corporate taxes in return for a lower interest rate on the bailout funds, a move that would make Ireland less attractive to investors and divert more business growth to the countries that are providing the bailout money. This would put Ireland between a rock and a hard place since the country needs more business investment to rebuild its economy. Once the fox is in the henhouse, none of the chickens are safe.

Ireland's banking collapse has triggered the largest emigration of Irish since the potato famine that caused so many to move to America in the 1840s.[19] With unemployment expected to reach 16 per cent, many breadwinners are simply leaving their families to work overseas.

Portugal was the next to fall. Despite months of claiming it would not accept a European Union bailout—which comes with provisions that limit a government's ability to control its own economy—by April 2011 Portugal had agreed to accept a $110-billion package conditional on spending cuts, tax increases, and privatization of some government assets and services.

These collapses are ignored in Canada on the premise that they are small economies, but the differences between them and us are only time and amount. We are following exactly the same path, and the result is somewhat inevitable without real changes.

Larger European countries that recognize this danger have already started to make the necessary changes. Spain is next in line for collapse. Its economy is larger than those of Greece, Ireland, and Portugal combined. Spain's government is the union-backed Spanish Socialist Workers' Party. Despite this strong connection, the Party passed laws to reduce the power of unions and implemented a series of austerity moves to reduce spending. Spain has the added burden of a 20 per cent unemployment rate, the highest in Europe. The country's economic growth is predicted to be less than 1 per cent in 2011,[20] offering no hope of the "higher revenues" that failing governments—such as Canada's—hold out as the solution to their endless deficits and mounting debt. Spaniards responded with a general strike on September 29, 2010, which included fires in the streets of Barcelona, but there is no other way out for Spain.

In France, 1.2 million people joined one of five nationwide strikes in October 2010 as workers protested the government's plan to raise the retirement age from 60 to 62. Strike-related disruptions led to cancelled flights and trains, closed ports, stopped the fuel industry, and brought France to a standstill for several days but had no affect on the government's decision, which is designed to salvage the pension system by saving on two years' worth of payments. At 62, France would still have the lowest retirement age in the developed world. In Canada there is talk of raising the retirement age to 67 for CPP, OAS, and GIS eligibility. Of course that would not affect those in the bell jar—government workers and politicians who cut their own deals to receive pensions after a specific period of service, regardless of age.

In the United Kingdom, a $128-billion budget cutback over four years will see the loss of up to 500,000 public sector jobs, the biggest fiscal tightening since World War II.[21] England intends to cut $28.5 billion in welfare payments, child benefits, and public housing, and raise its retirement age to 66.

The U.S. of A.

And then there's the U.S. of A. This is a story much closer to home. The U.S. economy suffers from the same maturation disease that we have—an older, less productive, and more expensive workforce that makes it unattractive to industry. Even its own companies are choosing not to invest there. A study by the Business Roundtable and the United States Council Foundation,[22] an American trade and commerce think tank, found that the percentage of profits of U.S.-based multinational companies that came from their foreign holdings had increased from only 17 per cent in 1977 to 48.6 per cent in 2006. President Barack Obama, noting that U.S. companies are sitting on $2 trillion in assets, has asked them to invest in the U.S., but it is unlikely that this will happen as long as other countries are more appealing (which will probably be the case for the next 50 years). Official unemployment remains above 9 per cent, but many credible economists say the real rate is 16 per cent to 22 per cent,[23] meaning there are less people with money to spend on consumer goods, which would stimulate the economy. Meanwhile, both public and personal debt are at record highs.

Canada's debt levels are at record highs. What are Canadian politicians doing about this? Having elections and promising more spending. Oh yes—and promising to stop deficit financing in a few years, but not right now. The federal debt under the Conservatives' 2011 election promises is expected to increase by $172 billion over the next four years before it miraculously balances. The federal Conservatives say they will balance the budget without raising taxes or cutting services. That would be a magic trick of epic proportions. Even the government's own parliamentary budget officer, Kevin Page, doesn't think this is going to happen, saying we have a "structural deficit"—meaning one that is built into the process and can't be eliminated—of $10 billion per year.[24]

9

A TEN-STEP PLAN FOR PENSION REFORM

There's also a strong and growing sense of unfairness among work-
ers who don't work in the public sector, two-thirds of whom don't
have any kind of company pension plan. Many of those who do have
company plans have seen them converted to defined-contribution
(DC) plans, wherein the size of their pension depends on what the
invested funds provide at retirement. Implementation of this pay-as-
you-go type of plan is the only way to get government pension costs
under control.

Gwyn Morgan, *The Globe and Mail*

As we have seen so far in this book, and as its title suggests, the system
of pensions that has been created for Canada's public sector is no longer
sustainable. It was developed with the idealistic goal that retired public
sector workers in Canada should have a disposable income close to their
final salaries.

Pensions were originally designed to protect workers from the possibility of living in poverty during retirement. Such protection is an admirable
goal for society, and one that we support. The combination of the Old Age
Security program, the Guaranteed Income Supplement, and the Canada
Pension Plan, in addition to RRSPs, provides this for many Canadians, and
these programs should certainly be tweaked to better provide for those
seniors who are still struggling financially. Public sector unions, however,
have negotiated pensions that lift their retired members far above the poverty line. Their plans have been heavily funded by Canadian taxpayers and
provide a seamless level of income support for public sector employees,

spanning their careers and continuing into their retirement until death. In fact, many retirees on public sector plans have a higher disposable income in retirement than they had on average during their working years. It is unfair for taxpayers to be on the hook for these liabilities.

Public sector pensions have traditionally been defined benefit plans. This is consistent across Canada and throughout the Western world. There has been a serious lack of discussion in Canada about public sector pension reform, but other governments have begun to address the issue. The UK, California, and Rhode Island have finished in-depth analyses to uncover systemic problems in public sector pensions and identify the best options to correct pension-related problems going forward.

The UK reforms are based on policies developed by Lord Hutton, the former Labour Party Business Secretary, with a very moderate and liberal political perspective. Many of the Hutton Report[1] findings coincide with the Little Hoover Commission's[2] report into public sector pensions in California. Finally, a report from the Treasurer of the State of Rhode Island,[3] built upon the UK and California findings, may provide the most comprehensive solutions to public sector pension reform. The fight to make pensions sustainable and fully funded by employee contributions, rather than relying on constant additional cash injections from taxpayers, is essential, and a battle that taxpayers must win. Based on an analysis of these reports we present this road map for solving Canada's pension predicament.

A Ten-Step Plan for Public Sector Pension Reform

1. Change the retirement age.

The most immediate change that needs to be made is to realign the retirement age of the public sector with that of private sector Canadians. We recommend public sector pensions use the established CPP age (currently 65) as the basis for determining the retirement age for public sector workers. If early retirement (between 60 and 65) takes place, there should be a reduction in pension benefits that corresponds to the reductions in place for early retirement under the CPP system.[4] This should also be applied to workers in so-called "public safety" careers, who are allowed to retire five years earlier than everyone else. If they are not physically capable of performing the tasks of a safety officer, they should be transferred to a less physically demanding job to complete their public service careers, or retire with a reduced pension.

A realignment of public sector worker retirement ages with social security norms was recommended in the Hutton Report. According to a 2008 StatsCan study, "Federal Public Service Retirements: Trends in the New Millennium," Canada's public sector employees retire earlier than any other in the world. The study notes that while the average age of retirement within the Canadian labour force in general is close to 62, in the public sector, 58 has been the average age of retirement over the last decade. In 2005, the average age of retirement from the public sector in the European Union was 60.9, with Iceland (66.3) and Ireland (64.1) boasting the highest retirement ages. The next lowest retirement ages were France (58.8) and Slovenia (58.5). In the U.S., 27 major federal agencies of the United States averaged a retirement age of 58.7.

2. Eliminate the CPP Bridge Benefit and OPEBs.

This is a special arrangement that allows public sector retirees to collect full CPP benefits during early retirement prior to age 65. Public sector retirees should be subject to the same CPP regulations as all other contributors.

This should also apply to extending health care benefits to early retirees. Currently, many early retirees continue to receive the full benefit packages received by those still working, often at no cost. There has been virtually no examination of the liability of OPEBs in Canada. These benefits could potentially be as large as unfunded pension liability deficits.[5]

3. Base Pensions on Career Average Earnings.

Current public sector pensions boost payouts by allowing members to use their highest three or five years' income as the base for pension benefit calculations. Private sector DB pension plans use lifetime career average incomes. This change would make pensions more sustainable and reduce the risk of future shortfalls.

4. Eliminate Buyback Options.

Many pension plans allow members to make one-time contributions to the fund in lieu of actually working. This is in reality a guaranteed investment program, since the taxpayer guarantees the rate of return. Since the plans have insufficient money to pay the higher benefits, this is essentially a form of larceny that—again—gives public sector workers more money than they deserve. All working Canadians have access to the RRSP and the TFSA programs. If a public sector worker has additional funds to invest in his own retirement, these funds should be invested privately. Taxpayers are already on the hook for the pension earned by the worker; they should not also be subsidizing pensions for service time not worked.

5. Eliminate Double-Dipping.

Changing the retirement age would go a long way toward controlling double-dipping, but legislation ensuring that no public sector worker can be paid a pension and a public sector salary at the same time should be enacted. If a person is qualified to retire but chooses to continue working, her pension should be put on hold until she does retire. If she chooses a lower-paying job—perhaps through a sense of duty, or a desire to remain active and contribute her skills to the public good—a partial pension benefit could be given to raise her total income to the level of her previous job, but she should not make more in "retirement" than she did when she was working.

6. Eliminate Pension Spiking.

Overtime pay should not be included in pension calculations. Overtime is already compensated at higher rates than regular hours, so the benefit is given as the work is done—it should not be used as a credit toward higher lifetime pensions. In return, pension contributions would not be charged on overtime earnings.[6]

Taxpayers need to ensure that there are no other termination benefits such as sick-time payouts, vacation payouts, or termination allowances that go toward the calculation of final pension benefits.

7. Cap Pension Earnings.

As we have seen, the Income Tax Act specifically limits government pensions to $101,161 (in 2008) including CPP, based on an annual income of $144,516.00,[7] adjusted annually. The Supplementary or Supplemental Executive or Employee Retirement Plans (SERP),[8,9] created by and for public sector employees who earn more than this to circumvent this legislation, eliminated the pension ceiling for public sector employees. This was highly unethical considering that the beneficiaries almost certainly knew that their contributions would not come close to funding the benefit payments they would receive. SERP is one of the best examples of the most powerful public sector employees abusing their power. Why should taxpayers subsidize already overpaid civil servants? Higher-income earners can fund their own RRSP or TFSA for higher pension benefits.

The State of Illinois, facing the same fiscal calamity from public sector pensions, introduced House Bill 146[10] in 2011. It places limits on the pensions that senior bureaucrats and managers receive. The bill would apply a $106,800 maximum-salary basis for calculating the pensions of its workers. Canada's SERPs should be cancelled immediately, and the Income Tax Act enforced for all government pensions.

The Illinois law applies to new pensioners, but existing pensions could be clawed back through progressive taxation. It would be possible, for instance, to create a reasonable ceiling, say the average income of a single Canadian—currently about $41,000 per year—and have publicly-funded pension income above that amount taxed at a much higher level. As an example, let's suggest that the first $25,000 after the annual ceiling would be taxed at 50 per cent, the next $25,000 above that at 75 per cent, and any pensionable income above $91,000 per year would be taxed at 90 per cent. This recovered pension income should be put directly into the Canada Pension Plan or redistributed through the OAS and GIS programs, which could then be raised for those at the bottom income levels.

8. Standardize Accrual Rates.

All public sector employees are important. The practice of boosting accrual rates to allow some to retire earlier than others is inherently unfair to those who must work longer before retiring. We might, on the surface, feel that a police officer is more important than a garbage dump worker, but if you were to spend time in either job you would quickly realize that being a police officer might be preferable to spending eight hours at a smelly dump every day. Multiply the daily unpleasantness of working at a dump by 35 years and it becomes reasonable to suggest that the dump worker should be allowed to retire earlier than the officer. Either way, society cannot operate properly without both. Officers already receive higher pay with its related benefits and pensions. All public sector pensions should be based on the same accrual rate. We suggest this rate should be 1.25 per cent, which for a 40-year career would result in a pension that replaces 50 per cent of income, or if a slightly higher rate is sustainable, at 1.5 per cent.

9. Change Future Pensions to DC or Hybrid Plans.

It will be difficult to go from a DB plan to a full DC plan in one step. We have seen around the world that any adjustment to pensions generates monumental battles between government workers and any politicians who have accepted the challenge of protecting the taxpayer. Wisconsin public sector protests and those in the UK, Greece, and France saw millions of government workers shut down services and stage angry protests. It might be more politically acceptable to phase in the transition by first creating a "hybrid" plan that combines features of DB and DC pensions. Originating in the Little Hoover report from California, the DB portion of a hybrid pension plan provides the base for retirement and the DC plan is "stacked" on top. This seems to be the most viable option for pension reform today. In July of 2011 the City of Atlanta in Georgia implemented this plan for its city workers' pensions.[11]

A hybrid plan would create a fair distribution of risk between the employee and taxpayers. Currently in the public sector the general accrual rate is 2 per cent. Our recommendation is to change this to a rate of 1 per cent for the defined benefit portion of the pension and 1 per cent for the defined contribution portion. The employer would be responsible for the DB portion and employee contributions would go into the DC portion.

As an example, employees with a $30,000 annual pension would have $15,000 coming from the DB portion and $15,000 from the DC portion of the pension. If the investment assumptions made by the plan managers are correct there would be no change to the pension benefits. If there are funding shortfalls, they would be the responsibility of current employees and not the responsibility of future taxpayers.

Currently government managers who negotiate DB plans have a clear conflict of interest because they ultimately receive the same benefits they promise to government employees. A DC plan would provide transparency of the compensation promises made and the funding situation, along with any financial consequences for taxpayers.

At the point the hybrid plan is introduced all employees, new and existing, would start accumulating under the new hybrid plan. Changes would occur on a go-forward basis so that all current employees currently enrolled in DB plans would have accumulated credits from the old plan "vested." This means that existing contracts would be honoured up until the current date but that new contributions from taxpayers and employees would go into the new system. For example, if an employee has worked 20 years under the existing DB plan they would be entitled to 40 per cent (20 years $\times$ 2% accrual rate) of the wage estimated for pension benefits. This would be their vested rights. From this point on all pensions would accrue under the hybrid system. All new pensions vesting would happen under the new plan.

10. Create a Comprehensive Public Report.

Politicians are reluctant to talk about public sector pensions and are deathly afraid of them arising as a political issue. They have so far thwarted any attempt to make these pensions an election issue. Perhaps, as Dan Kelly of the Canadian Federation of Independent Business says: "No wonder politicians won't deal with gold-plated public service pensions. Taxpayers pay $5.50 for every $1 from MPs in their platinum plan."[12]

It is a travesty that, leading up to pension reforms at the end of 2010, all levels of government had commissioned special task forces, expert commissions, and special reports to examine retirement security in private sector Canada. While these commissions and reports all examined retirement planning from a broad perspective, they did not even check the heartbeat of the 800-pound gorilla sitting in the corner, public sector pensions. When you consider how much of our country's wealth is now under the control of these pension funds, it is stunning to consider that no government has been willing to investigate their management, goals, and sustainability. Only a groundswell of public anger will cause a review. Look at the assets of some of the largest of these plans:

Table 9.1: Largest pension plans in Canada (based on most recent annual report information)[13]

	Members	Assets ($ billion)
Ontario Teachers' Pension Plan (OTPP)	295,000	107.5
Federal—Public Sector Pension Investment Board (PSP Investments)	561,000	58
Ontario Municipal Employees Retirement System (OMERS)	409,000	53
Quebec Government and Public Employees Retirement Plan	45,010	41.3
Healthcare of Ontario Pension Plan (HOOPP)	257,712	35
B.C. Municipal Pension Fund	267,000	27
Alberta—Local Authorities Pension Plan (LAPP)	206,000	17.6
Ontario Public Service Pension Plan (PSPP)	77,924	17
B.C. Teachers' Pension Plan	77,000	16
Total	**2,195,646***	**332**
CPP Investment Board (CPP)	17,000,000	148.2

*Includes active and retired members

The first place to start the reform of our pension system is with a federally commissioned investigation to uncover the details about public sector pensions in Canada. A good place to start would be to use the terms of reference set out for the Hutton Report:[14]

- the growing disparity between public service and private sector pension provision, in the context of the overall reward package—including the impact on labour market mobility between public and private sectors and pensions as a barrier to greater plurality of provision of public services;
- the needs of public service employers in terms of recruitment and retention;
- the need to ensure that future provision is fair across the workforce;
- how risk should be shared between the taxpayer and employee;
- which organizations should have access to public service schemes;

- implementation and transitional arrangements for any recommendations; and
- wider government policy to encourage adequate saving for retirement and longer working lives.

Not only are pensions confusing to elected officials, but they can be extremely confusing to average Canadians who have never had any exposure to them. It is important for all Canadians to hold politicians and unions accountable. There must be a basic understanding of pension-related concepts, and we have a created a checklist for all Canadians to use—including politicians, employers, and taxpayers—to evaluate the various pensions in place at each level of government. Although most pensions are similar in many ways, there are differences within each one, depending on how successful a given union has been in negotiating concessions.

Checklist for Pension Accountability

- Retirement age: At what age can employees retire (50, 55, 60, 65)?
- Change from DB to DC or hybrid: Have substantive changes been contemplated? Have any been enacted?
- Accrual rate: What is the accrual rate—2 per cent, 2.33 per cent?
- Salary calculation: Is it the final five years, highest salary, or career average?
- Pension caps: Is there a cap in place or is there a SERP?
- Pension spiking: Are overtime, sick time and vacation payouts, and retirement bonuses used in final pension calculations?
- Pension buybacks: Can pension-eligible time be purchased?
- Early CPP: Does the plan offer a bridge benefit?
- Double-dipping: Can employees collect pensions while working elsewhere?
- What portion of the plan is funded by taxpayers? Fifty, 75, or 100 per cent? What is the cost of taxpayer contributions?
- Is the pension fund underfunded? (This can be discovered by looking at the fund's financial report.)

- How much did the taxpayer have to "top up" the fund with additional contributions last year? The year before?
- What is the total projected deficit of the fund?
- What are the pensions of the politicians who negotiated this contract? Do they enjoy the same or similar provisions?

By asking your area politicians these questions you can bring the unfairness of public sector pensions to the forefront of their agendas. If your elected representatives can't answer these questions, you will know that they don't understand the problem or are trying to cover it up. Make your position clear and ask them to investigate those pensions under their jurisdiction—municipal, provincial, and federal. Send your local representatives a copy of this book with a covering letter. Through massive country-wide effort, we can bring this 800-pound gorilla into the open and begin the reforms necessary to make pensions sustainable and fair.

Naturally we would expect public sector unions to be actively supporting existing plans and fighting against changes, however, they need to consider the risk presented by the status quo. There is a very high likelihood that delays in making the changes necessary to ensure a sustainable pension system will have a greater negative effect on retirees in the future than any short-term unpleasantness such changes might cause. New employees will be in the system for another 35 years. Pensions will have melted down long before that point if taxpayers decide they are no longer willing to fund existing DB pension promises.

Consider the Saskatchewan Teachers Superannuation (pension) Plan. As of June 30, 2010, the unfunded liability in the Teachers' Plan is estimated—by their own managers—to be $4.006 billion.[15] At that date there were 1,499 active teachers contributing and 11,280 people receiving pension benefits from the Commission. The fund has only $999 million in assets.[16] To balance this fund the working teachers would have to contribute $2.6 million each. Hope they can attract the "best and the brightest" to take care of this without taxpayer support. (Don't hold your breath.) Based on the fact that the fund is currently paying pension benefits of $309 million per year, the fund will be bankrupt by 2014. After this time the shortfalls will be the sole responsibility of taxpayers. This will then be known as a "pay as you go" plan.

This colossal failure of plan management has occured despite extremely conservative goals of a 3.3 per cent yearly return, which they exceeded, having achieved 5.2 per cent over the past 10 years, so it has been clear for decades that the contribution rates by employees were not remotely sufficient to fund the pension guarantees negotiated by their union and agreed to by the local education boards and the Provincial Legislature. This same taxpayer ripoff has occurred with virtually every public sector pension fund in every jurisdiction in Canada. With their own retirements imperilled and the future debt of the gold-plated pensions of the protected class being heaped upon their children and grandchildren, it will be only a matter of time before taxpayers stage their own protests.

10

STEERING THE *TITANIC*

Societies . . . are no longer judged by their economic prowess in terms of their growth, but by the extent by which they take care of their bottom 10 per cent
Dr. Atif Kuburski, Econometric Research Limited

In 1912 the day's greatest engineers built a ship that represented the best of modern civilization. The world's elite lined up for the maiden voyage of this unsinkable marvel, but as we know, the results were disastrous. The *Titanic*, a pinnacle of man's achievements, was destroyed by one of nature's most basic elements—frozen water. The ship's captain ignored warning signs, thinking the *Titanic* was simply too big to fail. One hundred years later, Western civilization, the pinnacle of human society, is heading for a similar fate. Will our captains heed the warning and change the course of our ship?

The pension Ponzi we have outlined in this book is the tip of the iceberg; lurking below its surface is the public sector economy and the massive public debt it is built upon. Together they are growing ever larger, and if we do not change our course, they will sink us all.

Canadians have been lulled into a false sense of security by countless studies claiming that this is the best country in the world in which to live. We don't disagree, but point out that our envious position in the world order has been paid for with $1 trillion of debt and is therefore unsustainable. This is exactly what happened in Iceland, which until 2008 had one of the highest standards of living in Europe, built on borrowed money. Small country, big debt—just like Canada. Ireland had the fastest-growing economy in Europe, built on credit and artificially low business taxation. Five of its six banks collapsed, with the last one surviving only because of government bailout. Greece worked with disgraced U.S. financiers at Goldman Sachs to hide its massive debt until after acceptance into the European Union. Once the real numbers were discovered, Greece was faced with crippling debt restructuring, massive public sector layoffs, pension cuts, and higher taxes on everyone for years to come. This story is being repeated throughout the Western world, including the mighty U.S. which postponed financial default for another year by borrowing billions more to raise its $14.3 billion "debt ceiling" in July 2011.

The Real Economic Story

Economists, journalists, and politicians use the term "gross domestic product" (GDP) in reference to Canada's economic health relative to other countries. However, this concept offers a distorted representation of our economy's strength and a false sense of security when considering our future. The GDP is, in simple terms, the market value of all goods and services *produced and consumed* in a country over a certain period of time, including consumer purchases, government spending, new investment in industrial production, and the net value of exports over imports. If you are simply borrowing money to buy more things, this is not a sign of real growth in the economy.

Since World War II, developed economies have been driven by consumer purchases. Prior to the 2008 recession, 70 per cent of the North American economy was based on this. In the boom years of the '60s and '70s, this consumption was driven by higher incomes generated through manufacturing—which is true economic growth—but in the past 20 years, more and more of it has been driven by easy credit, which has led to record debt at both the personal and government level. When the GDP rises, as it does almost every year, it is assumed that the country is prospering. This makes sense on the surface, but a closer look shows that the GDP does not differentiate between wealth-creating (or goods-producing) and wealth-consuming activity within our economy—which is merely the recirculating of existing money.

Here's an example. If you invest $2 in a tomato plant and sell the tomatoes for $10, that would be recorded as $12 of GDP. If you then take that $10 and get your hair cut we have $22 in GDP. If the barber buys a used book for $10 we now have $32 in GDP and so on. But in reality we have only $8 in real growth (the profit on the tomatoes) with the remaining $24 being recirculated money. To build a wealthier country with a higher standard of living requires an economy weighted toward goods-producing activity. Historically this was the case for Canada, with its resource-based economy and strong dependency on heavy manufacturing. Today, however, our wealth creation is far outweighed by our wealth-consuming (service-producing) activities.

FIGURE 10.1 Manufacturing Share of GDP in Selected Countries

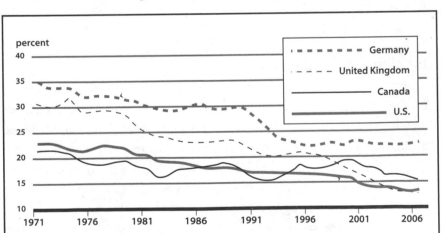

Sources: Statistics Canada; U.S. Bureau of Economic Analysis; United Kingdom Office for National Statistics; Organisation for Economic Co-operation and Development; Department of Finance Calculations

Western economies are shifting from a manufacturing base to a service based economy as reflected in their GDP numbers. This is a move from a wealth-creating society to a wealth-consuming one. The growth of the public sector is accelerating this transfer and is being supported by ever-expanding government debt. It is unsustainable, and will eventually force a correction, as we are currently seeing in Greece, Ireland and other European countries.

The financial services industry is our leading private employer, second only to our governments. The contribution of both industries to our GDP is 100 per cent recirculated money. Our growing public and service-based sectors creates a higher GDP, but this number reflects recycled money (wealth consuming) for such expenditures as financial planning fees, pensions, health care, and teacher's salaries and not true economic growth. Canada has traditionally been called a "resource-based economy" but we are now largely a nation of paper pushers. It is sobering to consider that less than 7 per cent of our GDP now comes from oil, gas, and mining. From 2006 to 2010 our total GDP increased from $1.191 trillion to $1.233 trillion (up 4 per cent)[1] but the goods producing sector declined from $370 million to $344 million (down 7.3 per cent).[2] This economic shift shows no sign of reversing, and eventually it will become impossible for those in wealth-creation to generate enough money to support the public sector and retirees at their current levels of income.

So, where do we go from here? How do we change the direction of the *Titanic*?

Thinking Outside the Box

What if we could start from scratch and redesign our system completely? The first thing we need to do is reduce the cost of our public sector. We don't believe that this problem can be fixed with a few minor tweaks. We have to laugh when Ontario Finance Minister Dwight Duncan says he's going to trim Ontario's $19-billion deficit (and $200-billion debt) by eliminating perks such as free golf club and gym memberships for public servants. That's like trying to empty Lake Ontario with a bucket.

Our elected representatives have no realistic plan to fix the debt problem. In fact, they don't seem to even recognize that there is a problem. Listen to this statement by retiring Auditor General Sheila Fraser in May 2011 on the challenges of balancing the federal budget: "It could be an increase in taxes, it could be a reduction in programs, but there's really only two areas you can work on to be able to balance the budget—*unless we decide we're going to leave a debt for our children and grandchildren.*"[3] (Italics ours.)

Fraser, who is retiring at 60 and presumably has children and grand-children, seems blissfully unaware—despite 10 years of examining the country's financial accounts—that she already is in fact leaving her offspring with a huge debt—a $1.2 trillion debt that grows every day. Today's politicians count it as a great win when they can reduce the yearly deficit. And we don't mean eliminate it, just reduce it! The federal Tories are bragging about balancing the budget in four to five years. The media makes that sound as if we will be out of debt by then. The truth, as you know by now, is that they are talking about the yearly deficit—the amount added to the accumulated debt from past deficits. No one—we repeat—NO ONE has a plan to eliminate the debt. Doing so is virtually inconceivable in our current system.

Why do we accept deficit budgets? What if each level of government set its budget as last year's revenue and divided the pie according to a set formula? For instance, the government might decide to spend 5 per cent on the military, 20 per cent on debt interest, 25 per cent on health care, 30 per cent on education, 5 per cent on foreign aid, and so on, and earmark, say, 5 per cent for debt reduction. Each department could plan its year based on its budget. These percentages could be realigned every few years, but would always result in a balanced budget. Surplus revenue each year would be used to reduce the debt. An increase in revenue would cause an increase in spending for the next year, but this would include increased debt reduction as well. As the debt went down, interest payments would shrink, and this would also increase the amount that could be spent. Government department managers would provide the best service possible with their budgets.

We believe our governments must come clean about finding solutions to our fiscal dilemma and not continue to paper over it with with mean-ingless statements about balancing the budget without any tax increases or service cuts while true costs continue to escalate every year. As Sheila Fraser clearly says, there is no other way. The first and most obvious step is to reduce the compensation costs of the public sector. This includes salaries, benefits and of course pensions. Public sector unions have sold us on the mantra that we must pay more to attract the "best and the brightest" to the public sector, but in reality we need those people driving our wealth-creating economy in the private sector, not using their talent to create an ever-larger debt load for the rest of us to pay. We believe public sector compensation costs are out of control and need to be reined in. Some recovery could be achieved through higher income taxes, such as those we recommend in Chapter 9 on pension income. Lower costs could be achieved through salary cuts if existing workers are willing to take less to keep their jobs (unlikely), but we expect it will require actual job cuts. This would seem to indicate a cut in services, but with creative thinking we can minimize service reductions.

It is time to examine ALL facets of the civil service and find ways to provide services at a lower cost. Every department, including community services, public transit, police, utilities, the military, healthcare and education needs to be redesigned for a leaner more sustainable future, instead of the current focus on maintaining and expanding the existing structure. Since more than 50 per cent of all government spending is on human resources, it is essential that we find ways to cut these costs.

Consider our school system as an example. In Alberta, student enrolment increased from 2001 to 2009 by only 2 per cent, but the number of educators rose by 9.4 per cent. Provincial spending on education increased from 2002 to 2012 by 63 per cent. Alberta now spends about $11,611 per student funding its K–12 school system,[4] with an average class size of 16 students. Compensation costs for salaries, benefits, and pensions account for 76 per cent of the Calgary's school budget.

An OECD report shows that, with the exception of Luxemburg, Canada's teachers are the highest paid in the world.[5] The OECD average starting salary for teachers is $28,949. In B.C. it's $47,000. Compare this with the U.S. at $35,999, the UK at $30,534, and France at $23,735. The same applies for the average top-of-career salary of $75,000 for B.C. teachers, compared to the OECD average of $48,022, the U.S. with $50,922, the UK with $44,630, and France with $47,108. Pensions add another 40 per cent onto actual salary compensation, meaning that an average senior teacher will cost taxpayers over $100,000 per year. A fully-qualified teacher is eligible to retire at age 55 with a pension valued at over $50,000. B.C.'s student population has fallen about 9 per cent over 10 years but spending on classrooms has risen more than 75 per cent.

Could we perhaps use technology to provide education at a lower cost than the labour-intensive system we have today? Kids get much of their early education from television. Sesame Street taught an entire generation their ABCs, and Blue's Clues, Dora the Explorer, and other shows help develop our children's understanding of culture, friendship, and the world around them. But once they hit school, game over. It's textbooks, chalkboards, and lectures—things that most kids find deadly dull. Teenagers have access through the Internet to almost every piece of knowledge known to man. Why are we not encouraging home study to reduce the number of supervised teaching hours? Currently there is no interest within the system for changes that reduce teaching positions. Mary-Lou Donnelly, president of the Canadian Teachers' Federation told the *National Post*[6] that a more effective way to improve education would be to provide better working conditions for teachers—more time off for professional development, smaller class sizes, and increased resources for special needs students. More time off for employees who work only 38 weeks of the year?

What about the military? The military consumes about 10 per cent of federal government revenues—some $22 billion in 2011.[7] That's $60 million *a day*. At this rate we will spend more than $220 billion on the military in the next 10 years. This for a country with no real enemies that has not been invaded for 200 years. Is it money well spent?

Do we need 60,000 fully-trained fighters and 30,000 reserves in peacetime? Plus 28,000 administrators and support staff? The Afghan mission started with 100 troops and escalated as high as about 3,600 at any one time, less than 4 per cent of our army. A total of 41,000 enlisted Canadians spent some time in Afghanistan. If that was our war effort—the first in more than 50 years—did we really need an additional 50,000 at home? Is it time to ask the military to justify their budget to the taxpayers?

Health care remains our biggest single expense. According to a 2009 report from the Canadian Institute for Health Information,[8] an independent, not-for-profit corporation that provides essential information on Canada's health system, total health-care spending is almost $192 billion—about $5,600 for each man, woman, and child in the country. Seventy per cent of that comes from taxes, with the rest picked up by private insurance and out-of-pocket user fees. A C.D. Howe Institute report entitled "Chronic

Healthcare Spending Disease"[9] estimates the cost of our system will rise to $10,700 per person per year by 2031. Still think our health care is free?

Naturally we must look at salaries, and when we review the Sunshine List we see that the people at the top of our health care system are ranked right up there, compensation-wise, with university presidents. Dr. Robert S. Bell, CEO of the University Health Network, made $753,992[10] in 2010. If taxpayers are contributing 9 per cent into an employee pension on an income of $700,000, this adds $63,000 per year. Most CEOs will be taking away a full pension of 70 per cent, ($490,000 annually, in this case). For a $490,000 pension, about $8 million is required in present-day cash. If the CEO lives 25 years into retirement he will receive in excess of $12 million. Twelve million for a retired CEO? Still think health care is free? There is no way this plan can be fully funded by the time he retires, so the taxpayer will pay for it.

The same story, but with lower numbers, is found throughout our health care system. Ontario's Sunshine List includes radiation technologists, scientists, and numerous managers, with even some nurses and a priest now making more than $100,000—plus benefits, of course. Some of these people earn as much as $400,000 a year. Ron Sapsford, the former Ontario deputy health minister, was paid $762,000 the year *after* he resigned his job as temporary CEO of eHealth Ontario,[11] a $1 billion-program that failed to meet expectations.

Will our health care workers work for less? Will Canadians accept a lower level of services? Is there a better, less expensive way to provide health care—perhaps home care? Should we be investing money in prevention programs, rather than disease management, the current model? Should there be a higher user-pay penalty? Should there be some privatization allowed, or even encouraged? There can be no untouchable subjects if we are serious about preventing the collapse of our economic system.

We must privatize, consolidate, or simply pare down government services wherever possible. The public sector unions focus on preservation of jobs and expansion of budgets and departments: empire building. The private sector, as we know, operates on a different financial model: fiscal sustainability first and profits second. When things get tight, the private sector cuts back; the public sector simply borrows more money on your behalf. For these reasons, the private sector can always deliver products and services more efficiently than the public sector. And equally important, there will always be the pressure of competition in the private sector, which is non-existent in the civil service. Consolidation of under-utilized resources and paring down of overfunded ones would yield savings across the board.

Pensions Re-imagined

The focus of this book, however, is pensions, so let's leave these questions for another time. Can we think outside the box and contemplate a pension system that better reflects true Canadian values of fairness and equality? What if we were starting from scratch, knowing what we know today? Re-imagining our pension system allows us to consider any and all possibilities, and these next ideas challenge the very foundations of the status quo. In hindsight we can see the flaws in our current system. It's time for some "blue-sky thinking" options.

The employment-based pension system is clearly broken. What if we cancelled all work-based pensions in Canada, including the CPP? Is there a more equitable way of sharing our tax dollars? Can we end the disparity between those who qualify to reap the benefits of tax-deferred pensions and those who retire to an old age of financial insecurity?

The employment-based pension system is broken. In the private sector, defined benefit (DB) plans are being abandoned at every contract negotiation. In the public sector, existing funding models have destroyed any semblance of sustainability for their DB plans. Ending all of these plans—including the CPP—would end the tax-deferred retirement income system. The additional income taxes raised would help balance the budget. Consider where we would be if there had never been any public sector pensions. The $800 billion now in those funds could have remained in the federal treasury and our public debt would be billions lower.

What would our country's financial position be if there had never been an RRSP program? With some $700 billion in RRSPs (2008),[12] how much of our national debt is due to people avoiding taxes by sheltering income this way? As we have seen, the income needed to maximize RRSP contributions means that this program has largely benefited those with higher-than-average earnings. They have been able to shelter up to $22,000 annually, while those with lower incomes are fully taxed.

According to the Department of Finance, the federal government collected $47 billion in combined employee and employer contributions to the CPP in 2010. If we assume that 80 per cent of employment is in the private sector we can estimate that the private sector contributed $39 billion to the CPP. What if we ended the mandatory employee/employer CPP contributions? This would keep billions in the hands of private business where it can be invested in economic expansion and job creation.

A Unified Pension Plan

If we cancel the CPP, RRSPs and employment-related tax-deferred pension plans, what alternative would we be able to provide to retired Canadians? Perhaps our taxes could fund a "unified" pension program (UPP) to provide all Canadians with the same benefits, in the same way they provide universal health care and education? Is our pension system less important than our health care or education systems? Why do we allow some groups and individuals to create tax-subsidized pensions while denying that same benefit to others? UPP benefits could be based on an agreed-upon poverty line for seniors, and adjusted using the Consumer Price Index (CPI) and other area-rated factors such as apartment rents and property tax. Statistics Canada does not define the poverty line in Canada, but social service agencies currently peg it at about $18,000.[13] The goal would be to provide all seniors with the same quality of life—one that allows them to retain their dignity and health, and that we can be proud of as Canadians.

Where would the money for this program come from? How about taking the money our governments currently give to business? In return for canceling the $39 billion in CPP contributions, our governments could stop subsidizing business and instead use this money to fund non-work-based pensions for all Canadians. Governments at all levels regularly give billions of tax dollars to business, through tax breaks, low interest loans or outright grants. This is often called "corporate welfare." While corporate taxes have received a lot of attention recently, with public sector unions suggesting governments raise these taxes to fund their compensation agreements, little focus has been given to cash grants and business loans.

Consider this: In 2010, Bell Aliant, a subsidiary of BCE, Canada's largest telecommunications company, received $14.5 million of federal money and $32 million in Ontario provincial taxpayers money[14] to expand services in rural Ontario. BCE had 2010 revenues of $18.4 billion and profits of $2 billion. Do they need your money? Subsidies to Canada's oil and gas industry from 1996 to 2002 totaled $8.3 billion.[15] The oil industry received some $2 billion in grants in 2010,[16] while setting record high prices and earning record profits. And, of course, Canada's highly successful banking industry received a $69.4-billion bailout between 2008 and 2010[17] through the "Economic Action Plan," (EAP) the federal initiative to prevent a possible economic collapse. Officially this was termed an "exchange of assets," as the government purchased insured mortgages from the banks to provide them with $69 billion in cash. Translation: Our government borrowed $69 billion and added it to the debt, then gave it to banks so they could make more money. These mortgages will be "safe" investments as long as there is no significant downturn in real estate values, but they still beg the question: Why are we as taxpayers in the mortgage business? It's difficult to find out exactly how much tax money is given to business, but in 2010 the federal government alone spent $39.9 billion on various business assistance programs—not including the EAP bailout funds. Much of this was paid to the private sector, which, in turn, contributes to the CPP.

By ending CPP contributions from business and ending tax deductions for employment-based pensions, abolishing taxpayer-funded public sector pensions and corporate welfare programs, governments could streamline government services, rebalance taxation and provide the money for a fair and equitable pension program for all Canadians.

What is the risk of this proposed strategy? Canada's pension plans, including the CPP, have been lauded by international experts as being in better shape than those in other Western countries, but as we have seen, much of this is smoke and mirrors. The public sector pension funds are short at least $300 billion, and most of the money that is in them was borrowed anyway. The high regard given to our country simply shows how bad things are elsewhere.

The risk of the UPP is that its true cost would be visible each year, and Canadians would have to decide whether pension benefits are sustainable. Whereas today the CPP is essentially a DB plan with benefit guarantees, UPP benefits could be reduced if there were not enough money to pay for them. Politicians and voters would have to choose between competing priorities: maintaining pension levels or more money for teachers, fighter jets, economic summits?

Keep in mind that politicians are already making those decisions every year, and so far the choice has always been to fund higher public sector wages and pensions. We believe Canadians are largely unaware that this has been happening for as long as it has, but now you know where your money has been going and why governments will never be able to balance their budgets without massive, systemic change.

Another UPP variable might be retirement age. Ending early retirement in the public sector would dramatically reduce civil service expenses by decreasing retirement length and resulting pension payouts as well as employee turnover. These changes alone would save billions. If the expected UPP benefits were still unsustainable, then the retirement age could be raised. A pay-as-you-go UPP—one in which payments come from general revenue and not from borrowed funds that are set aside—might require a later retirement age to be feasible at desired benefit levels. Regardless, a UPP would be infinitely more fair than the jigsaw puzzle that is our current pension system.

Voluntary workplace pensions funded completely by workers could be used by those with sufficient income to top up their government plans. Unions could continue to offer employee pensions, but ones funded only by employees. Employers who contribute to employee pension plans should be denied tax exemptions for these contributions.

These suggestions are just a few of the hundreds of innovations that could change the way our taxes are spent. What is needed is a complete review of all aspects of government. Only an open mind and a focus on change for the better, rather than the preservation of the status quo, can get us out of this mess. It is time to break open the bell jar and build a sustainable system that can carry all Canadians into a bright future in a changing world. Failure to adapt will doom us to a generation of stagnation and disappointment. It's time to think outside the box.

What Can You Do to Protect Yourself?

We have written of the problem at the government level, but what about on a personal level? What can you do to protect yourself from the coming disintegration of our economic system? In every transition, every financial meltdown, every pendulum swing from left to right or right to left there are winners and losers. How can you position yourself to be a winner in the face of these local, provincial, national, and international trends? Let's consider some possibilities.

Take advantage of RRSPs, TFSAs, and/or RESPs. Given the state of our government finances it would be prudent to create your own retirement fund via an RRSP or a TFSA. If you have children, start a Registered Education Savings Plan. Like the TFSA, contributions are not tax deductible, but the government injects an automatic 20 per cent contribution annually, and the fund grows tax-free. If your child does not use the fund, it is available to you after his 25th birthday, at which time you can invest it elsewhere.

Join the winning side. If you can't beat them, join them. We would be remiss if we didn't suggest that you get a government job. We hope that a change is coming and that the overly-generous environment public sector unions have built for themselves will not last much longer. But as we write this there is nothing to suggest that our politicians have the vision, integrity, or courage to significantly change course. So we think a good option is to snag a government job and start building your own taxpayer-guaranteed pension income.

Become an entrepreneur. Most Canadians will need to earn more money to protect themselves in retirement. If you can't get a government job, and your current job doesn't offer a realistic option of increasing your income, start your own business. This is the route taken by many people who have been cut from the workforce, especially those over 50. Self-employment, however, is a minefield of challenges, so do your homework and choose wisely.

Leave the country. If you are nearing retirement age or have already retired and recognize that your pension income is not going to provide the lifestyle you anticipated, you may want to consider selling everything you have and moving to Panama, Costa Rica, or an other country with a low cost of living and low taxes. You will not be the first retired Canadian in these stable countries; large and growing numbers are there already, including retired civil servants, spending their tax-dollar pensions to support another country's economy. They will be the ones in the largest villas with the best views.

Move to Alberta or Saskatchewan. These two provinces are in the midst of an economic boom that shows no sign of slowing down.

What Does The Future Hold?

As the next generation of taxpayers realizes the financial burden it faces in supporting retirees, the anger against public sector workers will reach the point where it can no longer be ignored by politicians. We are witnessing— day by day—revelations in the media that expose the ineptitude, duplicity, and corruption of a political machine that has lost touch with the reality of life for most Canadians. In less stable countries these conditions lead to revolution in the streets. In a stable democracy, these conditions are the winds of change that swing our political pendulum from left to right and back again.

As the situation worsens, expect protests in the streets and many vitriolic discussions. Meanwhile, the burden grows ever greater on the shoulders of the next generation. Every day in Canada another 1,000 Canadians turn 65; this trend will continue until 2029. We have been hearing about this coming demographic shift since David Foot's visionary book, *Boom, Bust and Echo* was published in 1996. Now the demographic tsunami has reached our shores. The number of seniors over age 65 in Ontario alone will more than double from 1.8 million in 2010 to 4.1 million by 2036.[18] By 2017 there will be more people over the age of 65 than under the age of 14. Pensions will feel the crunch. For example, in 1979 there were 6.35 workers contributing into the B.C. Municipal Pension for every retiree. By 2009 that ratio had dropped to 2.72.[19]

We are witnessing a change slowly taking place from coast to coast. Harper's 2011 majority—the Conservative party's first in 19 years and only its third in 73 years—marks the rebuilding of a party that was reduced to a mere two seats in 1993. Despite the reality that the Conservatives have spent more than any other government in history, they are generally seen to support business and oppose labour unions. One of Harper's first moves was to order back-to-work legislation against striking postal and airline workers. While a strong NDP Opposition will oppose and nitpick Conservative policies, there is nothing it can do to stop Harper from pushing his agenda. If he is willing to extend his anti-union stance to the public sector he could correct the errors of the past in one term.

In the 2010 Ontario municipal elections we saw significant change in leadership as mayoral incumbents were turfed in record numbers, replaced in large part by new faces promising cutbacks in city staff and no increase in property taxes. Led by surprise winner Rob Ford in Toronto, voters seemed willing to support any reasonable call for fiscal accountability in municipal government. Despite his stop-the-gravy-train rhetoric, Ford's first announcement was that he would add 100 officers to the Toronto Police Service, a move that would cost the city some $630 million over the next 55 years. The police force graciously rejected the offer as unnecessary, and then negotiated a four-year, 11 per cent raise, making it the highest-paid force in the country and setting a new benchmark for other municipalities to match.

Ford's next target was garbage, but his efforts to privatize were limited by a union contract stipulating that any workers who lose their jobs through privatization must be given new jobs by the city at the same pay.

As governments demand more concessions from unions, we can expect strikes in every sector which allows strikes. We should expect work-to-rule campaigns, work stoppages, disruptions in service, and possibly even illegal strikes. We should expect union-financed media campaigns ominously predicting overcrowded schools, rampant crime, people dying in fires or in hospitals waiting for treatment, food shortages, unsafe water, and invasion by terrorists. Never is there talk about union-initiated changes to make the system better or more productive. (Authors' note: In July 2011, OPSEU president Warren Thomas referenced the Walkerton contaminated water tragedy to criticize Dalton

McGuinty's announcement of 1,900 public sector job cuts. "The lesson of the Mike Harris era is that cuts to public services hurt us all. . . . In 2003, Dalton McGuinty was elected to turn the page on eight years of destructive cuts that lead to the systemic collapse of many public services and contributed directly to the death of seven people in the Walkerton water tragedy. Those who ignore history are destined to repeat it."[20])

We will be bombarded with claims that the real problem lies in the corporate sector and that businesses should pay higher taxes in order to provide Canadians with the exceptional service we expect. There will be suggestions that governments have slipped their private sector cronies billions of dollars that should, instead, have gone into government services. We will be told that our rank-and-file public sector employees are underpaid and overworked, and we will hear stories of real people who toil in public sector jobs saving lives and sacrificing for the good of the taxpayers. And when these tactics fail to stop the swinging pendulum, the unions will turn on the very politicians and bureaucrats who have so far been their staunchest allies. Unions will revert to their traditional worker-versus-management role and claim that there is not enough money because of administrative inefficiency. They will target highly-paid middle and upper managers in the public sector and expose the waste that we all know is there, and that they are in the best position to reveal.

Unions will be right about a few things. But this fight is not about being right; it's about correcting a wrong that has been going on for 40 years. It's about the fact that Canada has been digging itself into a financial hole so deep that we can barely see the light of the sky above us anymore. It's about the fact that our current political system is run by politicians who are either unable or unwilling to run our country within its financial means, or else are so self-centered or oblivious that they shun their responsibilities as our elected representatives whenever necessary to ensure they are re-elected and receive a lifetime pension for a few years in office.

This fight is about a governing system that is no longer focused on serving the people but rather has become a relentlessly expanding organism that focuses on feeding itself, becoming ever larger, ever more cumbersome, ever more expensive, and ever less efficient.

It is clear that public sector employees are not yet on board with reform of the system and its attendant loss of jobs, income, and benefits. For them, there is no problem with pensions. Pensions are an entitlement they believe is earned by virtue of working for the government. They see a bottomless pot of money, and have no interest in the problems of the rest of the country unless these problems threaten their own bottom line.

We have seen enormous protests in the U.S. and Europe because of these issues. A 48-hour general strike in Greece in June 2011 protesting pension cuts, privatization of government services, higher income taxes, and large-scale layoffs in the public sector left over 300 injured as rioters pelted projectiles at police, who responded with tear gas. The same month hundreds of thousands of public sector workers in the UK, including teachers and police, walked out for 24 hours to protest a $130-billion cut in public spending that will cost many careers and require workers to contribute more to their pensions. These protests have been repeated in France, which raised its retirement age from 60 to 62. The first serious demonstration in North America occurred in the state of Wisconsin in 2011. It was estimated that 40,000 public sector employees took to the streets to protest moves by the governor to end the collective bargaining power of some public sector unions. Democrats actually left the state to try to prevent the legislation and had to be brought back by police to fulfill their elected duty.

What is interesting about these protests is that they are not led by taxpayers, but rather by unionized public sector workers, protesting austerity measures worldwide as governments threaten to reduce the public sector workforce to try and rein in massive debts and future liabilities. Politicians are fighting unions on our behalf, but the groundswell of support they must be hoping for has not yet fully emerged. On the other hand, the public's traditional support of unions against their employers has also not been evident. Perhaps taxpayers will finally realize that they are, in fact, the employer, and that every perk and benefit, every salary and pension increase, every expansion of the public sector payroll diminishes their own disposable income and reduces the money available for the government services they expect.

According to the Bank of Canada, our average inflation rate as measured by the Consumer Price Index[21] has been 2.1 per cent over the past 20 years.

Public sector compensation packages have typically targeted 3 per cent as the minimum yearly raise. With merit and salary grid advancements, coupled with increased benefits and pensions, these 3 per cent increases average 4–5 per cent in real value. As an example, a $50,000 salary increasing at 2.1 per cent annually for 20 years would result in a final year salary of $75,767. At 3 per cent annually, the final salary would be 19 per cent higher at $90,305. At 5 per cent the salary increases to $132,664, or 75 per cent more than the CPI justifies. As a recent study by the Frontier Centre for Public Policy[22] found, wages of federal public administration workers grew by 59 per cent between 1998 and 2009, twice as much as across the entire economy. It is time that the public sector fell in line with the rest of Canada. The indexing of CPP pensions for 2011 (the amount of this year's increase in benefits) is set at 1.7 per cent. Why not have public sector compensation packages increase at the same rate as the CPP?

Will That Be Cash Or Credit?

The best way to consider proposed expenditures and budget increases at all levels of government, as well as salary increases in the public sector, is to ask: will that be cash or credit? And the answer will always be credit, because all of our governments currently spend more than they bring in.

So imagine that every new request is going on your personal credit card. Sixty-five F-35 fighter jets for $28 billion—would you put that on your credit card? Subsidized day care, hosting the G20 economic summit, the national gun registry—at $1 billion each—would you put any of that on your card? Farewell gift of $1.4 million to a retiring university president— credit okay? A $12 million pension for a hospital CEO? When you realize that every new expenditure will be financed with borrowed money that you—and your kids—will have to pay back, it changes your perception as to what we should be doing with our funds.

We'd like to see that kind of thought process at the table when budgets are being discussed. Right now that's not happening. About any and all of the outrageous waste of tax dollars mentioned in this book, politicians will merely say, "Well, it wasn't really that much—just a billion here, 25 million there, 300 billion there. It was in the budget." We mentioned earlier that Canadians consider government spending and government debt to be the government's problem, not theirs. Well, the government sees all of this debt as *your* problem. Politicians are happy to continue spending whatever it takes for them to stay employed and retire happy, because they don't have to pay it back—remember, it's going on your credit card.

The Final Word

Let's see if we can put this into sound bites for you.

Western economies are failing to compete globally, saddled with massive public debt, burgeoning governments, an aging workforce, and an unsustainable standard of living. The future will likely feature continuous austerity at all levels as developed countries—Canada included—begin to pay back a combined debt load estimated by *The Economist* at $40 trillion[23] and growing by $1 million every 12 seconds. Or they can simply default and send the world into an inflation spiral the likes of which has never been seen.

Canada's GDP shows that our wealth-consuming sector has been outpacing our wealth-creating sector for the past decade and this trend is not going away. This means there is less "real money" in our system each year.

The demographic shift of the retiring baby boom, long expected but never properly planned for, is here to stay. Nothing will be the same as it was when the boomers were productive.

A large portion of the wealth in our country is in the hands of public sector pension plans and private RRSPs. This is tax-deferred income and is largely responsible for our government debt. Unless we find a way to recover this money, financial equality in Canada will remain an unrealized myth.

This book, *Pension Ponzi*, is the canary in the mine. Our public sector pensions, plus the lucrative employment contracts they are based on, are unsustainable, and are simply the tip of the iceberg in a Western economy built on borrowed time and borrowed money. It is time for all Canadians to make a choice about our country: are we all in this together, or is it every man for himself? Do we care enough about each other to rebalance our pension systems to make them fair for everyone, or will we continue to allow those lucky enough to find themselves inside the bell jar to live a better life at the expense of those outside? How we answer these questions will define us as a nation.

ENDNOTES

Introduction

1. National Post, "The Model That's Killing Pension Plans," http://www
.nationalpost.com/opinion/columnists/story.html?id=47d6e4ce-000b-4b0d-
8d70-fcf74065fff1 (accessed July 5, 2011).

2. Canadian Federation of Independent Business (CFIB), Wage Watch,
December 2008, http://www.cfib.ca/research/reports/rr3077.pdf (accessed
July 22, 2011).

3. Ontario Teachers' Pension Plan, "Teachers at a Glance," http://www.otpp.com/
wps/wcm/connect/otpp_en/Home/Corporate+Info/Teachers+at+a+Glance/
(accessed July 22, 2011).

4. OMERS, http://www.omers.com/ (accessed July 22, 2011).

5. CPP Investment Board, http://www.cppib.ca/ (accessed July 22, 2011).

6. The Globe and Mail, "Smoothing Changes Save OTPP from a $35-billion
Shortfall," April 8, 2011, http://www.theglobeandmail.com/globe-investor/
investment-ideas/streetwise/smoothing-changes-save-otpp-from-a-35-billion-
shortfall/article1976211/ (accessed July 22, 2011).

7. OMERS Pension Site, Member Newsletter, "OMERS Funding Strategy Right on
Course," Member News, Number 91, Summer 2011, http://www.omers.com/
pension/OMERS_Funding_Srategy_Right_on_Course.aspx (accessed July 22, 2011).

8. The City of Hamilton, Financial Report 2009, http://www.hamilton.ca/NR/
rdonlyres/5D8DCD38-518C-4F51-83FC-06AFD2A83967/0/2009FinancialReport_
rev8202010.pdf (accessed July 22, 2011).

9. Joey Coleman, "Ontario Universities Get Temporary Pension Relief,"
GlobeCampus.ca, August 5, 2010, http://www.globecampus.ca/blogs/
colemans-campus/2010/08/05/ontario-universities-get-temporary-pension-
relief/ (accessed July 22, 2011).

10. The Economist, "World Debt Comparison, The Global Debt Clock," http://
www.economist.com/content/global_debt_clock (accessed July 22, 2011).

11. Ibid.

12. Most of our references in the book will be in Canadian dollars.

13. Ibid.

14. Ibid.

15. Reuters, "Nortel's Pension Deficit Helped Push It Over Edge," January 19, 2009, http://in.reuters.com/article/2009/01/19/idINIndia-37522320090119 (accessed July 22, 2011).

16. The Toronto Sun, "Air Canada Unions Face Headwind on Defined Pension Benefits?" June 14, 2011, http://www.torontosun.com/2011/06/14/air-canada-unions-face-headwind-on-defined-pension-benefits (accessed July 22, 2011).

17. Google Finance, "The S&P/TSX Composite Index Had a Posted Rate of Return From January 1, 2008 to July 22, 2011 of -.75%," http://www.google.ca/finance?q=TSE:OSPTX,CVE:OSPVX (accessed July 22, 2011).

18. James Pierlot, "A Pension in Every Pot: Better Pensions for More Canadians," C.D. Howe Institute, 2008, http://cdhowe.org/a-pension-in-every-pot-better-pensions-for-more-canadians/4656 (accessed July 22, 2011).

Chapter 1

1. The Canadian Taxpayers Federation, "MPs Cash in on $116 Million in Pension & Severance Bonanza," May 3, 2011, http://taxpayer.com/node/14377 (accessed July 22, 2011).

2. Ibid.

3. The Vancouver Sun, "Double-dipping: Defeated MP Gets Severance Pay and a Senator's Paycheque," May 2, 2011, http://www.vancouversun.com/news/Double+dipping+Defeated+gets+severance+senator+paycheque/4821793/story.html (accessed July 22, 2011).

4. The Canadian Taxpayers Federation, "MPs Cash in on $116 Million."

5. Statistics Canada, "Public Sector Employment, Seasonally Adjusted, (Quarterly) (Canada)," May 27, 2011, http://www40.statcan.gc.ca/l01/cst01/govt65a-eng.htm (accessed July 5, 2011).

6. Alexandre Laurin and William B.P. Robson, "Supersized Superannuation: The Startling Fair-Value Cost of Federal Government Pensions: 2009," The C.D. Howe Institute, http://cdhowe.org/supersized-superannuation-the-startling-fair-value-cost-of-federal-government-pensions/4551 (accessed July 22, 2011).

7. CBC News, "MPs' Pension Fund Grew Amid Recession: Report," April 7, 2010, http://www.cbc.ca/news/canada/story/2010/04/07/mp-pension-fund.html (accessed July 22, 2011).

8. StatsCan reports that the total value of public sector pension funds in Canada, in 2007, was estimated at $606 billion in the regular public sector

pensions and $199 billion in the GCRA (government consolidated revenue arrangements). This total of over $805 billion has not yet returned to this level because of poor stock market performance. The GRCA are described as "public sector retirement compensation arrangements. These supplementary employee retirement plans were set up to provide pension benefits to senior employees beyond the maximum permitted registered pension plan benefits as set out in the *Income Tax Act*." Source: Statistics Canada, "Pensions Assets By Type of Plan at Market Value," http://www.statcan.gc.ca/pub/13-605-x/2008002/t/5213171-eng.htm (accessed July 22, 2011).

9. Department of Finance Canada, "Fiscal Reference Tables October 2010," October 12, 2010, http://www.fin.gc.ca/frt-trf/2010/frt-trf-10-eng.asp (accessed July 5, 2011). These tables show the federal gross debt at $883.3 billion and the total provincial debt at $388.3 billion.

10. We say 30 years because most of the accumulation in these funds has occurred in the past 30 years. StatsCan reports that the value of the two public sector pension accounts in 1990 was at $200 billion.

11. As of April 2011, Canada had an estimated population of 34,349,200. Divide the $1.2 trillion by this amount and it is $34,935.

12. Ted Mallet and Queenie Wong, "Wage Watch," Canadian Federation of Independent Business, December 2008, http://www.cfib-fcei.ca/english/research/canada/112-labour_policy/32-wage_watch.html (accessed July 5, 2011).

13. Frontier Centre for Public Policy, "Public Administration Wage Growth, Comparing Rates of Wage Growth in Industries across the Canadian Economy (1998–2009)," Ben Eisen, Senior Policy Analyst, http://www.fcpp.org/publication.php/3626 (accessed July 22, 2011).

14. City of Toronto, "2009 Financial Report, 2009 Consolidated Financial Statements," http://www.toronto.ca/finance/financial_reports.htm (accessed July 22, 2011).

15. Hydro One, "2010 Annual Report, 2010 MD&A and Consolidated Financial Statements," http://www.hydroone.com/InvestorRelations/Pages/AnnualReports.aspx (accessed July 22, 2011).

16. Ben Eisen, "Public Administration Wage Growth," Frontier Centre for Public Policy, February 16, 2011, http://www.fcpp.org/publication.php/3626 (accessed July 5, 2011).

17. Statistics Canada, "Pension Assets."

18. Canadian Federation of Independent Business (CFIB), "Canada's Pension Predicament," January 2007, http://www.cfib-fcei.ca/english/research/

canada/114-social_policy/182-canada_s_pension_predicament.html (accessed July 22, 2011).

19. Government of Canada, "Your Public Service Pensions and Benefits Glossary," July 4, 2011, http://www.pensionetavantages-pensionandbenefits.gc.ca/ glssr-eng.html (accessed July 5, 2011).

20. This is based on the typical accrual rate for public sector pensions. This is 2 per cent for each year worked, so after 35 years this is 70 per cent of income (35 × 2 per cent). Another 15 years at 2 per cent is another 30 per cent of income.

21. Many protection services jobs (police, fire, etc.) come with an accelerated accrual rate of 2.33 per cent. Therefore, a 30-year employee times the 2.33 per cent accrual makes a 69.9 per cent pension.

22. Hernando DeSoto, "The Power of the Poor," http://www.thepowerofthepoor .com/concepts/c2.php (accessed July 22, 2011).

Chapter 2

1. Twenty-five per cent of earned income up to the Year's Maximum Pensionable Earnings limit (YMPE), which was $48,300 in 2011.

2. Service Canada, "Canada Pension Plan—Payment Rates, January–December 2011," June 30, 2011, http://www.servicecanada.gc.ca/eng/isp/pub/factsheets/ rates.shtml (accessed July 5, 2011).

3. The Montreal Gazette, "City Hall Is Right to Get Tough on Pension Funds", July 4, 2011, http://www.montrealgazette.com/business/City+hall+right+ tough+pension+funds/5044299/story.html (accessed July 22, 2011).

4. Service Canada, "Canada Pension Plan Statement of Contributions," March 31, 2011, http://www.servicecanada.gc.ca/eng/isp/common/proceed/socinfo .shtml (accessed July 5, 2011).

5. CPP Investment Board, "2011 Annual Report, 2011 Annual Report Summary," http://www.cppib.ca/Publications/annual_report.html (accessed July 22, 2011).

6. Google Finance, "S&P/TSX Composite Index September 1, 2000 to September 1, 2010, Total Rate of Return 7.99%," http://www.google.ca/ finance?q=TSE:OSPTX (accessed July 22, 2011).

7. University of British Columbia, "SPP Pension Fund, Net Rate of Return 2001 to 2010, 3.79%," http://www.pensions.ubc.ca/staff/ror.html (accessed July 22, 2011).

8. Yahoo Finance, "Nikkei 225 Reached a High of over 38,000 and by July 2011 Had Fallen to 10,132," July 22, 2011, http://finance.yahoo.com/echarts?s= ^N225+Interactive#chart1:symbol=^n225;range=my;indicator=volume; charttype=line;crosshair=on;ohlcvalues=0;logscale=off;source=undefined (accessed July 22, 2011).

9. At the time of writing, the Government of Canada had just commenced a consultation process into the PRPP to determine its design alternatives.

10. CBC News, "RRSP Contributions Fell in 2008," *CBC.ca*, November 16, 2009, http://www.cbc.ca/news/business/story/2009/11/16/rrsp-contribution-data-2008.html (accessed July 5, 2011).

11. Bill Tufts, "Fair Pensions for All," http://fairpensionsforall.net/ (accessed July 5, 2011).

12. Statistics Canada, "Pension Plans in Canada," May 9, 2011, http://www.statcan .gc.ca/daily-quotidien/110509/dq110509a-eng.htm (accessed July 5, 2011).

13. Nova Scotia Pension Agency, "Supplementary Employee Retirement Plan (SERP)," no date, http://www.novascotiapension.ca/publicserviceplan/ members/supplementaryemployeeretirementplanserp (accessed July 5, 2011).

14. Statistics Canada, "Pension Assets."

15. Ibid.

16. The B.C. Municipal Pension Plan had a 10-year rate of return in 2004 of 9.1 per cent; by 2009 it had dropped to 4.8 percent.

17. The QPP is identical in design to the CPP program. The recent budget recommended a significant hike in premiums to keep it viable. The changes implemented required premiums to rise from 9.9 per cent in 2011 (the same as CPP) to 10.8 per cent by 2017. Source: Province of Québec, "Budget 2011–2012: A Stronger Retirement Income System," http://www.budget.finances.gouv .qc.ca/Budget/2011–2012/index_en.asp (accessed July 22, 2011).

18. Ibid. The new savings plan will be a voluntary workplace administered plan. Employers will be required to deduct contributions from employees. Like the PRPP, it is designed to mimic the actual details of the plan; it will not be available until late 2011.

19. Fred Vettese provides an excellent analysis. Source: Fred Vettese, "Saving for Retirement II," Morneau Shepell, http://www.morneaushepell.com/index .aspx?m=publications&s=vision (accessed July 22, 2011).

20. Statistics Canada, "Distribution of Homeowners by Size of Mortgage Payment Relative to Disposable Income and Selected Characteristics," April 27, 2011, http://www.statcan.gc.ca/pub/75-001-x/2011002/tables-tableaux/11429/ tbl003-eng.htm (accessed July 5, 2011).

21. Statistics Canada, "Income of Retirement-age and Working-age Canadians: Accounting for Home Ownership," July 2010, http://www.statcan.gc.ca/pub/11f0027m/2010064/part-partie1-eng.htm (accessed July 22, 2011).

22. Jack M. Mintz, "Summary Report on Retirement Income Adequacy Research," Department of Finance Canada, December 16, 2009, http://www.fin.gc.ca/activty/pubs/pension/riar-narr-eng.asp (accessed July 5, 2011).

23. Fred Vettese, "Saving for Retirement II."

24. Ontario Teachers' Pension Plan, "Getting Your Pension Outside Canada," http://docs.otpp.com/NonResidentPenPaym.pdf (accessed July 22, 2011).

25. Jonathan Chevreau, "Six Things You Should Know about Pension Income Splitting," *National Post*, November 21, 2007, http://network.nationalpost .com/np/blogs/wealthyboomer/archive/2007/11/21/six-things-you-should-know-about-pension-income-splitting.aspx (accessed July 5, 2011).

Chapter 3

1. UFCW, "Facts about Unions," http://www.ufcw.ca/index.php?option=com_content&view=article&id=29%3Aabout-our-union&catid=12%3Ajoin&Itemid=49&lang=en#link3 (accessed July 22, 2011).

2. The Economist, "(Government) Workers of the World Unite! Public-sector Unions Have Had a Good Few Decades. Has Their Luck Run Out?" January 6, 2011 http://www.economist.com/node/17849199 (accessed July 22, 2011).

3. Ibid.

4. Ontario Public Service Employee's Union (OPSEU), "History of OPSEU," http://www.opseu.org/organizing/history_/1910.htm (accessed July 22, 2011).

5. The Economist, "(Government) Workers of the World Unite!"

6. Statistics Canada, "Public Sector Employment, Wages and Salaries, by Province and Territory," http://www40.statcan.ca/l01/cst01/govt62d-eng.htm (accessed July 26, 2011).

7. Statistics Canada, "Public Sector Employment, Wages and Salaries," May 27, 2011, http://www40.statcan.gc.ca/l01/cst01/govt54a-eng.htm (accessed July 5, 2011).

8. Statistics Canada, "Pension Plans in Canada, Table 1, Registered Pension Plan Membership by Sector and Type of Plan," http://www.statcan.gc.ca/daily-quotidien/110509/t110509a1-eng.htm (accessed July 26, 2011).

9. Global News, "Canadians Brace for Summer of Discontent," June 10, 2011, http://www.globalnews.ca/Canadians+brace+summer+discontent/4921121/story.html (accessed July 5, 2011).

10. Wikipedia, The Free Encyclopedia, "Canadian Union of Public Employees," http://en.wikipedia.org/wiki/Canadian_Union_of_Public_Employees (accessed July 26, 2011).

11. Canadian Union of Public Employees (CUPE), "Topics," http://cupe.ca/topics (accessed July 22, 2011).

12. Adrian Humphreys, "Ontario Teachers OK $60 Fee to Fight PCs' Tim Hudak," *National Post*, April 6, 2011, http://www.nationalpost.com/news/Ontario+teachers+fight+Hudak/4565075/story.html (accessed July 22, 2011).

13. Frank Klees, "Can Working Families Buy Provincial Election," *Mpp.on.com*, June 7, 2011, http://www.frank-klees.on.ca/Newsroom/familycoalition_000.htm (accessed July 22, 2011).

14. Ontariopc.com, "The Truth about Tim Hudak," http://ontariopc.com/truth/2011/04/27/working-families%E2%80%99-members-are-fear-mongering-about-the-ontario-pcs%E2%80%99-education-plan/ (accessed July 22, 2011).

15. Ontario Teachers' Pension Plan, "Pension Benefits History," http://www.otpp.com/wps/wcm/connect/otpp_en/home/plan+funding/history+and+reference/pension+benefits+history (accessed July 26, 2011).

16. Note: StatsCan shows that in 2010 the average wage was $22.28 per hour. Multiply this by a 40-hour work week then by 52 weeks to get the estimate. http://www40.statcan.gc.ca/l01/cst01/labr69a-eng.htm (accessed July 22, 2011).

17. James Pierlot, "A Pension in Every Pot," C.D. Howe Institute, November 2008, http://www.cdhowe.org/pdf/Commentary_275.pdf (accessed July 22, 2011).

18. Ibid.

19. Currently the life expectancy is age 82; however, this is increasing at a rate of four months per year. This is a conservative estimate as StatsCan currently reports that "on average, a 65-year-old man could expect to live an additional 18.1 years in 2005–2007, an increase of 2.0 years from the previous decade. A 65-year-old woman could expect to live an additional 21.3 years, up by 1.3 years. Source: Statistics Canada, "Life Expectancy at Birth and at Age 65 by Sex, Canada," http://www.statcan.gc.ca/daily-quotidien/100223/dq100223a-eng.htm (accessed July 22, 2011).

20. CBC News, "With 90 Teachers over 100 OTPP's Problem Is Clear," April 5, 2011, http://www.cbc.ca/fp/story/2011/04/05/4562403.html#ixzz1TFYUxZnt (accessed July 22, 2011).

21. Calgary Board of Education, "Financial Statements and Statistical Information, Year Ended, August 31, 2009," http://www.cbe.ab.ca/trustees/Budget/08-09Financials.pdf (accessed July 22, 2011).

22. Ontario Teachers' Pension Plan, "Plan, Funding Challenges," http://www.otpp .com/wps/wcm/connect/otpp_en/home/plan+funding/funding+challenges (accessed July 22, 2011).

23. Ontario Teachers' Pension Plan, "Funding Update," June 2011, http://docs.otpp .com/SRI/PDFs/TeacherAnnounce_EN_060311.pdf (accessed July 22, 2011).

24. Public Works and Government Services Canada, "Advantages," http://www .tpsgc-pwgsc.gc.ca/pension/act/rachat-buyback/avantages-advantages-eng .html (accessed July 22, 2011).

25. Healthcare Of Ontario Pension Plan (HOOPP), http://www.hoopp.com/ members/build/psp/ (accessed July 22, 2011).

26. OMERS, http://www.omers.com/ (accessed July 22, 2011).

27. City of Hamilton, "City of Hamilton Financial Report, 2009," http://www .hamilton.ca/NR/rdonlyres/5D8DCD38-518C-4F51-83FC-06AFD2A83967/ 0/2009FinancialReport_rev8202010.pdf (accessed July 5, 2011).

28. Note: This estimate is that of the authors. It should be alarming that this third-rail issue has not been analyzed by anyone in government, including the auditors who are supposed to be protecting taxpayers' interests. Oh yeah, the auditors get DB pensions as well.

29. City of Toronto, "Financial Reports & Statements, 2009 Financial Report," http://www.toronto.ca/finance/financial_reports.htm (accessed July 22, 2011).

30. Hydro One, "Annual Reports 2010 Annual Report," http://www.hydroone .com/InvestorRelations/Pages/AnnualReports.aspx (accessed July 22, 2011).

31. Ontario Power Generation (OPG), "Annual Report 2010," http://www.opg .com/news/reports/?path=Annual%20Reports (accessed July 22, 2011).

32. Alexandre Laurin and William Robson, C.D. Howe Institute, "The Public-Sector Pension Bubble: Time to Confront the Unmeasured Cost of Ottawa's Pensions," http://www.cdhowe.org/pdf/ebrief_108.pdf (accessed July 22, 2011).

33. Heather McLaughlin, "Time to Reform Public-sector Pensions, City Told, Chamber Says City's Defined-benefit Plan Is No Longer Viable," *The Daily Gleaner*, May 30, 2011, http://dailygleaner.canadaeast.com/news/article/ 1410630 (accessed July 22, 2011).

34. The City of Winnipeg, "Winnipeg Fire Paramedic Service Overtime and Sick Leave Audit," May 2009, http://www.winnipeg.ca/audit/pdfs/reports/ WFPSOvertime.pdf (accessed July 22, 2011).

35. International Association of Firefighters, "British Columbia Fire Fighters Achieve Breakthrough on Pensions," http://www.iaff.org/canada/Updates/ bc_233.htm (accessed July 22, 2011).

36. Note: Take the example of a protection services employee with 30 years of service. The lifetime pension contributions would have been based on a 2 per cent pension. At 30 years, the employees would get a pension of 60 per cent. As soon as the change takes place, they are eligible for a pension of 69.9 per cent. In 2011, the City of Montreal reported that an average pension for a police officer was $59,000 at age 53. Assume this is a 60 per cent pension and the pensions change to a 2.33 per cent accrual rates. The new pension would be worth $65,785. Assuming the employees lives for 30 years longer and the pension is indexed at 2 per cent, they would now collect $2.67 million. The old pension would pay out $2.39 million. Taxpayers are on the hook for the extra $280,000 in pension.

37. Larry Brown and Mike Waghorne, National Union of of Public and General Employees (NUPGE), "The Coming Demographic Shock," April 2005, http://www.nupge.ca/files/publications/Pensions%20Documents/ The_Coming_Demographic_Shock.pdf (accessed July 22, 2011).

38. Brian MacDonald, "Waiting for Defence Budget 2011/12," The Conference of Defence Associations, http://cda-cdai.ca/cda/uploads/cda/defbudget2011.pdf (accessed July 22, 2011).

39. Steven Greenhut, *Plunder*, The Forum Press, 2009.

40. Colby Cosh, "Should Firefighters Be Able to Work Seven Shifts a Month?" *MacLeans.ca*, January 7, 2011, http://ca.news.yahoo.com/should-firefighters-be-able-to-work-seven-shifts-a-month-.html (accessed July 22, 2011).

Chapter 4

1. CBC News, "$104K payout to City of Ottawa auditor upsets taxpayers," January 27, 2010, http://www.cbc.ca/news/canada/ottawa/story/2010/01/27/ ottawa-lalonde-pension-auditor.html (accessed August 31, 2011).

2. Kenyon Wallace, "Tax Staff to be paid $25M in Severance, Rehired—HST Changeover; Swap to Federal Jobs Will Cost Ontario $25M," *National Post*, March 12, 2010.

3. Ibid.

4. The Cape Bretoner, "Feds Recover $350,000 Fee from Dingwall-led Lobby Firm," March 29, 2010, http://www.thecapebretoner.ca/?p=2275 (accessed July 22, 2011).

5. CBC News, "Audit Backs Dingwall's Expense Claims," October 26, 2005, http://www.cbc.ca/news/canada/story/2005/10/26/dingwall051026.html (accessed July 22, 2011).

6. Ibid.

7. The Ottawa Citizen, "Martin Unfairly 'Sacrificed' Mint Boss Dingwall, Report Says," April 13, 2006, http://www.canada.com/ottawacitizen/news/story .html?id=a4876903-6551-4e32-8c76-eada1fea1bd7&k=49709 (accessed July 22, 2011).

8. Stephen Harper, "Statement on Dingwall Severance Package," February 4, 2006, http://www.conservative.ca/EN/1091/40454 (accessed August 31, 2011).

9. CBC News, "Integrity Watchdog Left with $534,000," March 4, 2011, http:// www.cbc.ca/m/touch/news/story/2011/03/04/pol-integrity-commissioner .html, (accessed July 22, 2011).

10. Ibid.

11. Sonya Bell, "Fired After Scathing Report, Ex-integrity Commissioner Expected on Parliament Hill," *The Ottawa Citizen*, March 10, 2011, http://www.ottawacitizen.com/story_print.html?id=4411906&sponsor= (accessed July 22, 2011).

12. The Canadian Taxpayers Federation, "Report on New Brunswick MLA Pensions, Salaries and Expenses," *Taxpayer.com*, September 15, 2010, http://taxpayer.com/atlantic/report-new-brunswick-mla-pensions-salaries-and-expenses (accessed July 22, 2011).

13. The Canadian Taxpayers Federation, "Reform MLA Pensions," *Taxpayer.com*, http://taxpayer.com/node/13055, (accessed July 22, 2011).

14. David Beers, "MLAs Sitting Pretty," *TheTycee.ca*, May 1, 2007, http://thetyee .ca/Bigstory/2007/05/01/Raise/ (accessed July 5, 2011).

15. Will McMartin, "Huge Pay Raises, The Silent Issue," *TheTyee.ca*, April 29, 2008, http://thetyee.ca/Views/2009/04/29/PayRaises/ (accessed July 5, 2011).

16. Will McMartin, "BC Health Spending Exploding? Don't Believe It," *TheTycee .ca*, February 9, 2007, http://thetyee.ca/Views/2007/02/19/HealthSpending/ (accessed July 5, 2011).

17. The Globe and Mail, "Aide Paid to Cut Trees on Senator's Personal Property, Court Hears," http://www.theglobeandmail.com/news/politics/aide-paid-to-cut-trees-on-senators-personal-property-court-hears/article1395107/ (accessed July 22, 2011).

18. The Globe and Mail, "Senator Raymond Lavigne Guilty of Fraud," March 11, 2011, http://www.theglobeandmail.com/news/politics/senator-raymond-lavigne-found-guilty-of-fraud/article1938615/ (accessed July 22, 2011).

Chapter 5

1. Canada Energy, "History of Ontario Hydro," http://www.canadaenergy.ca/index.php?hydro=ontario&direct=hydro (accessed July 22, 2011).

2. Dominion Bond Rating Service Limited, "HYDRO ONE INC.," September 6, 2000, http://www.regie-energie.qc.ca/audiences/3401-98/Req-revisee/Hqt-8/HQT8_document35.PDF (accessed July 22, 2011).

3. Ontario Power Authority, "About the Ontario Power Authority," http://archive.powerauthority.on.ca/Page.asp?PageID=861&SiteNodeID=118 (accessed July 22, 2011).

4. The Globe and Mail, "Ontario Power Generation Workers Get Wage Hike Despite McGuinty's Restraint Plan," March 15, 2011, http://m.theglobeandmail.com/news/politics/ontario-power-generation-workers-get-wage-hike-despite-mcguintys-restraint-plan/article1942064/?service=mobile (accessed July 22, 2011).

5. Hydro One, "Annual Reports, 2006–2010," http://www.hydroone.com/InvestorRelations/Pages/AnnualReports.aspx (accessed July 22, 2011).

6. Jonathan Jenkins, "Power Utility Too Fat, Overpaid, Board Says," *Toronto Sun*, March 11, 2011, http://www.torontosun.com/news/torontoandgta/2011/03/11/17585736.html (accessed July 5, 2011).

7. The Toronto Star, "Political Embarrassment behind Privatization Talk," January 10, 2010, http://www.thestar.com/comment/article/748415 (accessed July 22, 2011).

8. The Hamilton Spectator, "Hydro Rates Rising to Cover Overcharging Fines Ontario Energy Board Poised to Rule on 6.2% Hike," February 23, 2011, http://www.thespec.com/news/ontario/article/490868--hydro-rates-rising-to-cover-overcharging-fines (accessed July 22, 2011).

9. Parker Gallant, "Ontario's Power Trip: OPG Produces Report, Little Information," *Financial Post*, March 9, 2010, http://network.nationalpost.com/NP/blogs/fpcomment/archive/2010/03/09/opg-produces-report-little-information.aspx (accessed July 22, 2011).

10. Parker Gallant, "Ontario's Power Trip: No Relief in Sight from Rising Costs," *Financial Post*, March 8, 2011, http://opinion.financialpost.com/2011/03/08/no-relief-in-sight-from-rising-costs/ (accessed July 5, 2011).

11. Ibid.

12. Parker Gallant, "Ontario's Power Trip: OPG Produces Report, Little Information."

13. The Society of Energy Professionals, "Arbitrator Critiques Govt Policy, Awards OPG Raises," *The Society of Energy Professionals Newscast*,

February 4, 2011, http://www.thesociety.ca/pdfs/Cast/Snc10-04.pdf
(accessed July 5, 2011).

14. Ontario Ministry of Finance, "2010 Ontario Budget: FAQ: Public Sector
Compensation Restraint to Protect Public Services Act, 2010," January 10,
2011, http://www.fin.gov.on.ca/en/budget/ontariobudgets/2010/faq_march
.html (accessed July 5, 2011).

15. Ontario Power Generation, "Statement of Executive Compensation, Form
51-102F6," http://www.opg.com/investor/pdf/2009_ExecComp.pdf (accessed
July 22, 2011).

16. Ibid.

17. Canadian Press, "Ontario Lowering Salaries for Energy Executives," *Toronto.ctv
.ca*, June 265, 2007, http://toronto.ctv.ca/servlet/an/local/CTVNews/20070626/
ontario_hydro_salaries_070626?hub=TorontoHome (accessed July 5, 2011).

18. CBC News, "Former Hydro One CEO Disputes Allegations," July 26, 2002,
http://www.ctv.ca/servlet/ArticleNews/story/CTVNews/20020726/hydro_
one_clitheroe_020726?s_name=t&no_ads= (accessed July 22, 2011).

19. CBC News, "Hydro One CEO Eleanor Clitheroe Fired," July 22, 2002,
http://www.cbc.ca/news/business/story/2002/07/19/hydroone_020719.html
(accessed July 22, 2011).

20. CTV News, "Former CEO Sues Hydro One Over Pension," June 13, 2010,
http://toronto.ctv.ca/servlet/an/local/CTVNews/20100613/ceo-sues-pension-
100613/20100613/?hub=TorontoNewHome (accessed July 22, 2011).

Chapter 6

1. CTV Calgary, "$4.75 Million Retirement for U of C Pres," September 21, 2009,
http://calgary.ctv.ca/servlet/an/local/CTVNews/20090921/CGY_uofc_pension
_090921/20090921/?hub=CalgaryHome (accessed July 5, 2011).

2. Gauntlet News, "President's Salary Details Angers Campus," September 24,
2009, http://thegauntlet.ca/story/13819 (accessed July 22, 2011).

3. MacLeans.ca On Campus, "UCalgary to Cut 200 Jobs by the Fall," July 16,
2009, http://oncampus.macleans.ca/education/2009/07/16/u-calgary-to-cut-
200-jobs-by-the-fall/ (accessed July 22, 2011).

4. Canada MSN News, "'Handshake' behind U of C President's $4.5M Pension,"
October 2, 2009, http://news.ca.msn.com/top-stories/cbc-article.aspx?cp-
documentid=22037343 (accessed July 22, 2011).

5. Gauntlet News, "President's Salary Details Anger Campus."

6. Ibid.

7. Ibid.

8. CBC News, "Faculty Calls President's Pension 'Obscene,'" October 8, 2009, http://www.cbc.ca/news/canada/calgary/story/2009/10/08/calgary-president-pension-faculty-letter.html (accessed July 22, 2011).

9. Wade Hemsworth, "McMaster's George Highest-paid President," *The Hamilton Spectator*, April 1, 2009, http://www.thespec.com/news/business/article/90540--mcmaster-s-george-highest-paid-president, (accessed July 22, 2011).

10. MacLeans.ca On Campus, "President's $1.4-million Golden Handshake," June 26, 2008, http://oncampus.macleans.ca/education/2008/06/26/mcmaster-president-to-get-nearly-14-million-after-retirement/ (accessed July 22, 2011).

11. The Hamilton Spectator, "Secrecy Makes It All Worse," January 10, 2011, http://www.thespec.com/opinion/editorial/article/319545--secrecy-makes-it-all-worse (accessed July 22, 2011).

12. MacLeans.ca On Campus, "Hey, Where Did My Tuition Money Go?" October 30, 2008, http://oncampus.macleans.ca/education/2008/10/30/hey-where-did-my-tuition-money-go/ (accessed July 22, 2011).

13. Ministry of Finance, "Public Sector Salary Disclosure 2011 (Disclosure for 2010)," http://www.fin.gov.on.ca/en/publications/salarydisclosure/2011/ (accessed July 22, 2011).

14. MacLeans.ca On Campus, "The Million Dollar President," August 6, 2010, http://oncampus.macleans.ca/education/tag/university-salaries-2010/ (accessed July 22, 2011).

15. MacLeans.ca On Campus, "Knocking on the Glass Ceiling," April 9, 2010, http://oncampus.macleans.ca/education/tag/university-salaries-2010/ (accessed July 22, 2011).

16. Ibid.

17. The National Post, "Civil Servants on Sunshine List Jump," April 1, 2011, http://www.financialpost.com/related/topics/Civil+servants+sunshine+list+jump/4539777/story.html (accessed July 22, 2011).

18. McMaster University, "Annual Financial Report 2009/2010," http://www.mcmaster.ca/bms/pdf/mac-2010fs.pdf (accessed July 22, 2011).

19. University of Guelph, "2011/2012 Integrated Pan and Preliminary MTCU Operating Budget," http://www.fin.uoguelph.ca/sites/default/files/2011-2012%20Integrated%20Plan%20and%20Preliminary%20MTCU%20Operating%20Budget.pdf (accessed July 22, 2011).

20. The Globe and Mail Globe Campus, "Ontario Campus Employee Wages at Top of Class," April 3, 2009, http://www.globecampus.ca/in-the-news/article/ontario-campus-employee-wages-at-top-of-class/ (accessed July 22, 2011).

21. Janet Steffenhagen, "Surrey School District Official Gets a Record $614,382 Compensation," *Vancouver Sun*, December 28, 2010, http://www.canada.com/vancouversun/news/westcoastnews/story.html?id=960f3ab6-46f7-469a-8568-ee4f33bc50cb (accessed July 5, 2011).

22. Note: The introduction mentioned that the Teachers' Pension Plan was short $35.7 billion and it implemented an accounting change called "smoothing" to reduce the pension to $17.2 billion. There was no change in either the assets or the liabilities of the pension plan. Many question the transparency of using smoothing in pensions, but it sure reduced a political headache for politicians who would have to explain the shortfall. Where it was implemented in San Francisco the public defender stated, "It is like telling your spouse that you lost only $500 in Las Vegas instead of the $5,000 you actually lost, because you are spreading your losses over 10 years. Source: Boyd Erman, "Smoothing Changes Save OTPP from a $35-billion Shortfall," *The Globe and Mail*, April 8, 2011, http://www.theglobeandmail.com/globe-investor/investment-ideas/streetwise/smoothing-changes-save-otpp-from-a-35-billion-shortfall/article1976211/ (accessed July 22, 2011).

23. CBC News, "Ont. Teachers' Fund Warns of Shortfall," April 5, 2011, http://www.cbc.ca/news/business/story/2011/04/05/otpp-funding-shortfall.html (accessed Month day, year).

24. CBC News, "N.S. School Boards Face Budget Cuts, 'Board Members Are in Shock,'" October 29, 2010, http://www.cbc.ca/news/canada/nova-scotia/story/2010/10/29/ns-school-boards-budget-cuts.html (accessed July 22, 2011).

25. Ibid.

26. CBC News, "N.S. School Board Warns of 100s of Jobs Lost," January 14, 2011, http://www.cbc.ca/news/canada/ottawa/story/2011/01/14/ns-chignecto-school-board-cutbacks.html (accessed July 22, 2011).

27. Statistics Canada, "Tables," April 29, 2011, http://www.statcan.gc.ca/pub/81-582-x/2011001/t-c-g-eng.htm (accessed July 5, 2011).

28. Statistics Canada, "Table C.2.1, Full-time Equivalent Enrolments in Public Elementary and Secondary Schools, Canada, provinces and territories, 2001/2002 to 2008/2009," April 29, 2011, http://www.statcan.gc.ca/pub/81-582-x/2011001/tbl/tblc2.1-eng.htm (accessed July 5, 2011).

29. Statistics Canada, "Table C.2.2, Full-time Equivalent Educators in Public Elementary and Secondary Schools, Canada, Provinces and Territories, 2001/2002 to 2008/2009," April 29, 2011, http://www.statcan.gc.ca/pub/ 81-582-x/2011001/tbl/tblc2.2-eng.htm (accessed July 5, 2011).

30. Government of Alberta, "Budget 2011: Total Government Support to the K-12 Education System," http://education.alberta.ca/department/budget.aspx and http://budget2011.alberta.ca/newsroom/charts-graphs.pdf#page=7 (accessed July 5, 2011).

Chapter 7

1. Ken Peters, "Halton Crime Way Down, but Police Budget Way Up," *The Hamilton Spectator*, January 13, 2011, http://www.thespec.com/news/local/ article/473289--halton-crime-way-down-but-police-budget-way-up (accessed July 5, 2011).

2. Benefitspro, "Job Mobility among Younger Workers Requires Different Benefits Model," April 1, 2011, http://www.benefitspro.com/2011/04/01/ job-mobility-among-younger-workers-requires-differ (accessed July 22, 2011).

3. The Toronto Star, "Board Ratifies 11.5% Pay Hike for Police," June 9, 2011, http://www.thestar.com/news/crime/article/1006050--board-ratifies-11-5- pay-hike-for-police?bn=1 (accessed July 22, 2011).

4. In early 2010, OMERS was reporting a deficit on its pension of $9 billion. It has since been changed through the magic of smoothing to around $4.5 billion. Regarding the $9 billion, see source: The Ottawa Citizen, "Municipal Pension Shortfall Could Affect Property Taxes," September 22, 2010, http://www .ottawaupdate.com/municipal-pension-shortfall-could-affect-property-taxes/ (accessed July 22, 2011). Regarding the $4.5 billion, see source: Tara Perkins, "OMERS Boosts Return, Funding Deficit Swells," February 28, 2011, http://www .theglobeandmail.com/report-on-business/omers-boosts-return-funding-deficit- swells/article1923350/ (accessed July 22, 2011).

5. Joe Warmington, "T.O.'s Top Constable Gets $175Gs," *The Toronto Sun*, March 31, 2011, http://www.torontosun.com/news/columnists/joe_warmington/ 2011/03/31/17829996.html (accessed July 22, 2011).

6. Toronto Police Service, "Salary and Benefits," 2011, http://www.torontopolice .on.ca/careers/salaryandbenefits.php (accessed July 5, 2011).

7. Heather McLaughlin, "Pension Decision Angers Union Leaders, Overtime Won't Be Part of Pension Income Calculation, City Rules," *The Daily*

Gleaner, May 25, 2011, http://dailygleaner.canadaeast.com/ (accessed July 22, 2011).

8. CBC News, "Doug Ford Questions Scrutiny of Police Paid Duty," May 10, 2011, http://www.cbc.ca/news/canada/toronto/story/2011/05/10/ford-del-grande-paid-duty432.html (accessed July 22, 2011).

9. BC Pensions, Municipal Pension Plan, "Retirement Age, When Can I Retire?" http://www.pensionsbc.ca/portal/page/portal/pen_corp_home/mpp_home_page/mpp_pt_near_retire/mpp_pt_nr_information/ (accessed July 25, 2011); Government of Ontario, "Ten New Justices Of The Peace Appointed," October 12, 2010, http://news.ontario.ca/mag/en/2010/10/ten-new-justices-of-the-peace-appointed.html (accessed July 22, 2011).

10. Canada.com, "More Police Officers Earning $100,000, Salary Report Finds," March 25, 2008, http://www.canada.com/cityguides/toronto/story.html?id=6a7c36ee-f86a-4ac7-bf58-e5142d13f956&k=2983 (accessed July 22, 2011).

11. Toronto Police Accountability Coalition, *Bulletin* No. 41, April 15, 2008.

12. Antonella Artuso, "Police Forced To Delay Hiring Officers," *Toronto Sun*, March 9, 2010, http://www.torontosun.com/news/torontoandgta/2010/03/09/13174016.html (accessed July 22, 2011).

13. Ontario Ministry of Finance, "Salary Disclosure 2005 (Disclosure for 2004) Municipalities and Services," October 7, 2009, http://www.fin.gov.on.ca/en/publications/salarydisclosure/2005/munic05.html (accessed July 5, 2011).

14. Wikipedia, "Julian Fantino," http://en.wikipedia.org/wiki/Julian_Fantino (accessed July 22, 2011).

15. The National Post, "Civil Servants on Sunshine List Jump," April 1, 2011, http://www.financialpost.com/related/topics/Civil+servants+sunshine+list+jump/4539777/story.html (accessed July 22, 2011).

16. Ontario Municipal Employee Retirement OMERS, "Past Annual Reports, Report to Members 2004," http://69.46.127.69/Assets/about+omers+section/2004+RTM.pdf (accessed July 22, 2011).

17. Ontario Municipal Employee Retirement OMERS, "Annual Reports, Report to Members 2010," http://www.omers.com/corporate/corporate_annual_report.aspx (accessed July 22, 2011).

18. Based on the authors' estimated trend from analyzing the past 10 years of annual reports.

19. Tara Perkins, "OMERS Boosts Return, Funding Deficit Swells," *Globe and Mail*, April 6, 2011, http://www.theglobeandmail.com/report-on-business/omers-boosts-return-funding-deficit-swells/article1923350/ (accessed July 5, 2011).

20. Ontario Teachers Pension Plan, "Annual Report 2010," http://www.otpp.com/wps/wcm/connect/otpp_en/Home/Annual+Reporting/Annual+Report/ (accessed July 22, 2011).

21. Google Finance, "S&P/TSX Composite Index," July 28, 2011, http://www.google.ca/finance?q=TSE:OSPTX (accessed July 22, 2011).

22. The National Post, "Civil Servants on Sunshine List Jump."

23. Katie Rook, "Deputy Police Chief to Leave the Force for Position at Magna," *The Globe and Mail*, January 13, 2005.

Chapter 8

1. Department of Finance Canada, "Federal Support to Provinces and Territories," http://www.fin.gc.ca/fedprov/mtp-eng.asp (accessed July 27, 2011).

2. Department of Finance Canada, "Annual Financial Report of the Government of Canada Fiscal Year 2009–2010," http://www.fin.gc.ca/afr-rfa/2010/report-rapport-eng.asp#a2 (accessed July 27, 2011).

3. Department of Finance Canada, "Fiscal Reference Tables, Table 15," July 27, 2011, http://www.fin.gc.ca/frt-trf/2010/frt-trf-1003-eng.asp#tbl15 (accessed July 22, 2011).

4. Department of Finance Canada, "Fiscal Reference Tables."

5. These numbers use the net debt which includes only the actual cash borrowed to pay ongoing government finance and not the "long-term liabilities."

6. The Canadian Taxpayers Federation, "Debt History," http://www.debtclock.ca/index.php?option=com_content&view=article&id=45&Itemid=42 (accessed July 22, 2011).

7. Interest is paid only on the net portion of the country's debt load.

8. Ibid. In 2009–10 the total gross debt of the federal government was reported at $883.3 billion with a little over 33 million Canadians.

9. Department of Finance Canada, "Table 7 Expenses."

10. Of the total $388 billion, Quebec has $142.8 billion, Ontario has $193.6, and B.C. has $28.0 billion. Greece in 2011 had $374.2 billion; Portugal had $177.5 billion; and Ireland had $157.0 billion. Source: Department of Finance Canada, "Fiscal Reference Tables."

11. William Gairdner, *The Trouble with Canada . . . Still! A Citizen Speaks Out*, 2nd ed., Key Porter Books, 2010.

12. Ontario Ministry of Revenue, "Ontario Health Premium," http://www.rev.gov.on.ca/en/tax/healthpremium/index.html (accessed July 22, 2011).

13. Statistics Canada, "Labour Force Surverys, January 2011 and December 1999," http://www.statcan.gc.ca/daily-quotidien/000107/dq000107a-eng.htm, and http://www.statcan.gc.ca/daily-quotidien/110204/t110204a2-eng.htm (accessed July 22, 2011).

14. William Gairdner, *The Trouble with Canada*.

15. Stefania Moretti, "Canadian Consumer Debt Rises $1,000 Per Person," *The Toronto Sun*, June 1, 2011, http://www.torontosun.com/2011/06/01/canadian-consumer-debt-rises-1000-per-person (accessed July 22, 2011).

16. Arnold Schwarzenegger, "Public Pensions and Our Fiscal Future," *Wall Street Journal*, August 27, 2010.

17. CBC News, "Income Gaps Grow, as Canada's Have-Nots Get Left Behind," May 1, 2008, http://www.cbc.ca/news/business/story/2008/05/01/censusfeature.html (accessed July 22, 2011).

18. Financial News, "Ireland Eyes Up Its National Pension Reserve," November 25, 2010, http://www.efinancialnews.com/story/2010-11-25/ireland-eyes-up-its-national-pension-reserve (accessed July 22, 2011).

19. The Week, "Ireland's Exodus: By The Numbers," http://theweek.com/article/index/212558/irelands-exodus-by-the-numbers (accessed July 22, 2011).

20. Economics Newspaper, "The Bank of Spain Lowers 2011 Growth Forecast to 0.8%," no date, http://economicsnewspaper.com/policy/spain/the-bank-of-spain-lowers-2011-growth-forecast-to-0-8-7237.html (accessed July 22, 2011).

21. The Daily Mail, "500,000 Public Sector Jobs To Go: Danny Alexander Lets the Cat Out of the Bag on Spending Cuts," October 19, 2010, http://www.dailymail.co.uk/news/article-1321842/SPENDING-REVIEW-500-000-public-sector-jobs-Danny-Alexander-lets-cat-bag.html (accessed July 22, 2011).

22. Business Roundtable and the United States Council Foundation, "How U.S. Multinational Companies Strengthen the U.S. Economy," Spring 2009, http://www.uscib.org/docs/foundation_multinationals.pdf (accessed July 22, 2011).

23. The EUTimes, "Real U.S. Unemployment Rate May Be 22.1 percent for February," March 6, 2011, http://www.eutimes.net/2011/03/real-us-unemployment-rate-may-be-22-percent-for-february/ (accessed July 22, 2011).

24. McLeans.ca, "PBO Projects $10-billion Structural Deficit Parliamentary Budget Office Cites Demographic Changes as Budgetary Drains," February 15, 2011, http://www2.macleans.ca/2011/02/15/pbo-projects-10-billion-structural-deficit/ (accessed July 22, 2011).

Chapter 9

1. Officially called the Independent Public Service Pensions Commission. HM Treasury, "Independent Public Service Pensions Commission," http://www.hm-treasury.gov.uk/indreview_johnhutton_pensions.htm (accessed July 22, 2011).

2. Officially called the Public Pensions for Retirement Security (Report #204, February 2011), Little Hoover Commission. Source: HM Treasury, "Independent Public Service Pensions Commission."

3. Rhode Island, Office of the General Treasurer, "TRUTH IN NUMBERS, The Security and Sustainability of Rhode Island's Retirement System," June 1, 2011, http://www.treasury.ri.gov/secure-path-ri/ (accessed July 22, 2011).

4. The penalty for taking early CPP is 0.6% a month for each month before turning 65. Therefore a retiree at age 60 sees a reduction of 36%. It is not possible to take CPP before age 60. Source: Morningstar, "CPP stiffens penalties for early-bird applicants," http://www.morningstar.ca/globalhome/industry/news.asp?articleid=381015 (accessed July 22, 2011)

5. Girard Miller, "Misplaced Pension Hysteria: The Real Monster is OPEB, Not Pensions," GOVERNING, February 3, 2011, http://www.governing.com/columns/public-money/Misplaced-Pension-Hysteria.html (accessed July 22, 2011).

6. CBC News, "Fredericton approves pension reforms", May 25, 2011, http://www.cbc.ca/news/canada/new-brunswick/story/2011/05/25/nbwooside-fredericton-pensions-1130.html (accessed July 22, 2011).

7. Nova Scotia Pension Plan, "Nova Scotia Public Service Superannuation Plan," December 23, 2010, http://novascotiapension.ca/publicserviceplan (accessed July 22, 2011).

8. Nova Scotia Pension Agency, "Supplementary Employee Retirement Plan (SERP)," http://www.novascotiapension.ca/publicserviceplan/members/supplementaryemployeeretirementplanserp (accessed July 25, 2011).

9. McCarthy Tétrault, "How to Create a Better SERP: Part 1," November 30, 2007, http://www.mccarthy.ca/article_detail.aspx?id=3784 (accessed July 22, 2011). Note: The plan is called different variations as shown here.

10. Illinois Retirement Security Initiative, "Bill Would Impose Pension Reforms on Existing Participants," January 16, 2011, http://www.ilretirementsecurity.org/ (accessed July 22, 2011).

11. AJC, Atlanta News, "Pension overhaul allows Atlanta to reduce layoffs, restore services," June 30, 2011, http://www.ajc.com/news/atlanta/pension-overhaulallows-atlanta-994079.html (accessed July 22, 2011).

12. HM Treasury, "Independent Public Service Pensions Commission: Terms of Reference," http://www.hm-treasury.gov.uk/indreview_johnhutton_pensions_tor.htm (accessed July 22, 2011).

13. CFIB DanKelly, "No wonder . . .," June 9, 2011, https://twitter.com/#!/CFIB/status/78768699099713536 (accessed July 22, 2011).

14. All figures are posted by the pensions either on their web site or in annual reports as of year end 2010. At the end of 2009, the Top 100 pensions in Canada had $660.9 billion in assets. The first private sector pension on the plan is for Canadian National Railways with $14.1 billion in assets. Of the top 100, 47 belong to the private sector. The largest private sector plan by membership is the Canadian Commercial Workers Industry Pension Plan with $1.4 billion in assets for 290,000 workers. Source: Benefits Canada, "Top 100 Pension Funds Report: Northward Bound," June 23, 2010, http://www.benefitscanada.com/pensions/governance-law/top-100-pension-funds-report-northward-bound-6965 (accessed July 22, 2011).

15. Saskatchewan Teachers' Superannuation Commission, "Interesting Facts," http://www.stsc.gov.sk.ca/ (accessed July 22, 2011).

16. Saskatchewan Teachers' Superannuation Commission, "09-10 Annual Report," http://www.stsc.gov.sk.ca/publications/2009-10%20TSC%20Annual%20Report.pdf (accessed July 22, 2011).

Chapter 10

1. In linked 2002 dollars, to adjust for inflation. The market value of the expenditure-based GDP in Canada was $1.696 trillion in the first quarter of 2011. Source: Statistics Canada, "Gross Domestic Product, Expenditure-based (Quarterly)," http://www40.statcan.gc.ca/l01/cst01/gdps02a-eng.htm (accessed July 22, 2011).

2. Statistics Canada, "Gross Domestic Product at Basic Prices, by Industry (Chained 2002 Dollars)," http://www40.statcan.ca/l01/cst01/ECON41-eng.htm (accessed July 22, 2011).

3. Bruce Campion-Smith, "Auditor General Sheila Fraser's Swan Song: A Blunt Warning," *Toronto Star*, http://www.thestar.com/news/canada/politics/article/997047--auditorgeneral-s-swan-song-a-blunt-warning (accessed July 22, 2011).

4. Government of Alberta, "Budget and Business Plan (2011–14)," http://education.alberta.ca/department/budget.aspx (accessed July 28, 2011).

5. OECD, "Education at a Glance 2010: OECD Indicators," http://www.oecd .org/document/52/0,3746,en_2649_39263238_45897844_1_1_1_1,00.html (accessed August 31, 2011).

6. National Post editorial board, "Giving Better Teachers The Money They Deserve," *National Post*, January 5, 2011, http://fullcomment.nationalpost .com/2011/01/05/national-post-editorial-board-giving-better-teachers-the-money-they-deserve/ (accessed August 31, 2011).

7. Brian Stewart, "$30B Fighter Jets Just The Start of Defence-Spending Boom," *CBC News*, Apr 6, 2011, http://www.cbc.ca/news/canada/story/2011/04/06/ f-vp-brian-stewart-navy.html (accessed August 31, 2011).

8. Canadian Institute for Health Information, "National Health Expenditure Trends 1975 to 2009," http://secure.cihi.ca/cihiweb/products/National_ health_expenditure_trends_1975_to_2009_en.pdf (accessed August 31, 2011).

9. David A. Dodge and Richard Dion, "Chronic Healthcare Spending Disease: A Macro Diagnosis and Prognosis," *C.D. Howe Institute Commentary*, http:// www.cdhowe.org/pdf/Commentary_327.pdf (accessed August 31, 2011).

10. Rob Ferguson, "Reform Commission to Look at Hospital Pay," *Toronto Star*, April 1, 2011, http://www.thestar.com/news/canada/politics/article/967751-reform-commission-to-look-at-hospital-pay (accessed July 22, 2011).

11. Keith Leslie, "Former Ontario Deputy Made $762,000 One Year After Leaving," *The Globe and Mail*, April 4, 2011, http://www.theglobeandmail .com/news/national/ontario/former-ontario-deputy-made-762000-one-year-after-leaving/article1970559/ (accessed July 22, 2011).

12. In 2008 Canadians had $631 billion in RRSP's. We suspect those numbers are higher as a result of the stock market "recovery" but maybe not. TSX returns were down 9% for the first 7 months of 2011. Source: Statistics Canada, "Data Source for Chart 18.2 Pension Assets of Canadians," http://www .statcan.gc.ca/pub/11-402-x/2010000/chap/pensions/c-g/desc/desc02-eng .htm (accessed July 22, 2011).

13. Statistics Canada uses a figure of between $ 15,583 and $ 22,637 for 2010 depending on the community size of residency. Source: Statistics Canada, "Low Income Cut-offs (1992 Base) Before Tax," http://www.statcan.gc.ca/ pub/75f0002m/2011002/tbl/tbl02-eng.htm (accessed July 22, 2011).

14. Nishnawbe Aski Nation, "Government Partners for New Fibre Optics Network in Northern Ontario Communities," http://www.nanbroadband.ca/upload/ documents/media_11-19-2011.pdf (accessed July 22, 2011).

15. Green Party of Canada, "Removing Corporate Subsidies: Distorting the Market," http://greenparty.ca/node/13303 (accessed July 22, 2011).

16. The Canadian Press, "NDP Wants Cut in Oilsands Subsidies," CTV News, March 31, 2011, http://m.ctv.ca/topstories/20110331/ndp-layton-110331.html (accessed July 22, 2011).

17. Government of Canada, "Insured Mortgage Purchase Program," http://actionplan .gc.ca/initiatives/eng/index.asp?initiativeID=39&mode=2 (accessed July 28, 2011).

18. Ontario Ministry of Finance, "Ontario Population Projections Update," http:// www.fin.gov.on.ca/en/economy/demographics/projections/ (accessed July 22, 2011).

19. Municipal Pension Plan, "Municipal Pension Plan 2009 Annual Report," http://www.pensionsbc.ca/portal/page/portal/pencorpcontent/mpppage/ publications/annualreports/mpp_ar_2009_print.pdf (accessed July 22, 2011).

20. NUPGE, "McGuinty Begins Biggest Wave of Layoffs in Ontario since the Mike Harris era," http://www.nupge.ca/content/4408/mcguinty-begins-biggest-wave-layoffs-ontario-mike-harris-era (accessed July 22, 2011).

21. Rate Inflation, "Canada - Consumer Price Index (CPI) History," http://www .rateinflation.com/consumer-price-index/canada-historical-cpi.php?form=cancpi (accessed July 22, 2011).

22. Frontier Centre for Public Policy, "Backgrounder No. 89," January 2011, http://www.fcpp.org/files/1/FB089_PSWageGrowth_F3.pdf (accessed July 22, 2011).

23. The Economist, "World Debt Comparison, The Global Debt Clock," http:// www.economist.com/content/global_debt_clock (accessed July 22, 2011).

INDEX